To Enid

From

Colin Leach

19th June 2013

MAN'S DESTINY

COLIN LEACH

authorHOUSE®

AuthorHouse™
1663 Liberty Drive
Bloomington, IN 47403
www.authorhouse.com
Phone: 1-800-839-8640

Published by AuthorHouse 3/27/2013

ISBN: 978-1-4772-3934-6 (sc)
ISBN: 978-1-4772-3935-3 (hc)
ISBN: 978-1-4772-3936-0 (e)

Library of Congress Control Number: 2012919890

Contents

MAN'S PROGRESS, FUTURE AND DESTINY

INTRODUCTION

Shortly after the Second World War, there occurred an extraordinary conjunction of events. Scientists working for the US government successfully detonated a thermonuclear device (H-bomb), giving the Americans the lead in the nuclear arms race. The lead was short-lived, however, for on 20th August 1953, the USSR exploded its first H-bomb. This raised the prospect of a nuclear war between the opposing superpowers, but on that very same day Earth entered the Age of Aquarius which, according to astrologers, is a period of harmony and understanding.

This conjunction could not have been coincidental because certain factors came together at exactly the right moment to save mankind. Furthermore, scientists might have mastered nuclear technology and detonated nuclear devices much earlier. But that raises a fundamental question: why should it have proved so difficult to split the atom?

The answer to this question is the final event in the conjunction: nuclear weapons only became available when Man's overwhelming desire was for peace, not war.

If nuclear weapons could have been deployed by Stone Age Man, or incorporated into the arsenals of warlords such as Attila the Hun and Genghis Khan, then Man might have been obliterated, but instead the science could only be understood when he wanted no more wars.

The same applies to the exploration of space. If space travel had been possible in earlier times, Man would have endeavoured to establish an empire by conquering other planets and subjugating their inhabitants, but the science for spacecraft was only discovered after his outlook had become peaceful and he had sent messages into space showing goodwill towards other life-forms.

The meaning is clear: the nearer Man comes to achieving peace and harmony, the closer he comes to beginning the exploration of space.

Clearly these scientific discoveries had a scale of difficulty that effectively withheld them from Man until he could handle them responsibly. This cannot have been coincidental – someone had to assign the scale of difficulty – which means Man's progress is governed by a pre-ordained schedule.

The schedule clearly requires Man to explore space, but since he is only at the initial stage of space projects, he is only at an early stage of the schedule.

Everything Man has achieved was part of a greater plan. If we can discover this plan, then we will know our destiny!

Where do we begin? Clearly the plan concerns the universe, and that gives us an obvious starting-point: to examine the factors that gave rise to the current state of the universe. This, however, requires us to consider events that take us back to the beginning – to Genesis.

In The Beginning

Chapter One

God Creates Man

Part 1

Genesis opens with the words, "In the beginning God created the heaven and the earth," and subsequent verses show that this was the initial stage of an operation whereby God created the perfect environment for Man and then created Man. However, nowhere in the Bible does God say why He created Man, and this omission appears to validate the scientific view that Man evolved naturally from the primates.

However, there is a missing link between Man and the primates. The gap consists of Man's vastly greater intellect. Scientists are convinced that eventually a species will be found that bridges the gap, but they are wrong. Man is endowed with physical and mental properties that evolution could never have brought about. Evolution is a process that aims at securing the survival of species – this is its ultimate goal. Man is advanced, both physically and mentally, far beyond this limit. He must therefore have been created by a different process, and for a higher purpose.

We thus arrive at a logical basis for the description of the creative act in Genesis 2.7, which says, "God formed man from the dust of the ground, and breathed into his nostrils the breath of life." God confirmed that this description was correct, because in Genesis 3.19 He told Adam and Eve, "dust thou art, and unto dust thou shalt return," and this is the basis of the section in the Christian funeral service that reads, "earth to earth, ashes to ashes, dust to dust."

However, science has proved that neither the human body nor that of any other creature deteriorates in this manner. The body decomposes into organic material that can be recycled, therefore "dust" should be regarded as a symbol for organic material that was capable of producing Man. If we substitute "primates" for material, and say that God performed on them a series of operations including genetic modification, then we have reconciled the Genesis account with the fact that there is only 6% difference between our DNA and that of the primates.

Once we view Man as a product of genetic engineering, then we can see the truth behind another episode in the Genesis account, namely, God creating Eve by removing one of Adam's ribs, for it illustrates a scientific fact: at the genetic level, there is only one difference between male and female.

The female has two normal-looking pairs of X chromosomes, but the male has only one X chromosome partnered by a Y chromosome that carries few or no genes. The female therefore carries more genes than the male – is more complete than the male – and this is shown by Adam having to part with a rib in order to create Eve. The imagery could not be closer.

* * * * * * *

We have reconciled the Genesis account of Man's creation with scientific studies into comparative DNA, and this means we have to change its time-frame. Genesis began not in 4004 B.C., as Archbishop Ussher thought, but millions of years earlier.

Within this time-frame earliest Man evolved into modern Man, and Genesis not only traces his progress but also explains key stages in the evolutionary process that have baffled scientists.

God wanted Man to be exceptionally intelligent, but creating him from primate material had obvious drawbacks. Man first appeared approximately 5 million years ago, but 3 million years passed before he learnt to use bones as clubs. The length of time is explained, according to Robert Ardrey in *African Genesis*, by the need for Man to acquire new co-ordination, which necessarily entailed developments in the brain and nervous system similar to those found in modern man – clear evidence that God could not genetically modify a primate to meet His needs.

This brings us to the next stage in Man's evolution, *Homo erectus*, but he also proved to be inadequate. He did not discover how to make fire until 500,000 years ago, and 200,000 years passed before he made the first 'houses' of branches. Shortly after this, around 250,000 years ago, he evolved into *Homo sapiens.*

Scientists have been unable to account for the short time-span between these two crucial stages in Man's development, but everything is explained in Genesis.

Genesis 2.7 says the first Man was created from "dust," but we have already shown this to be primate material. Adam does not appear on the scene until Genesis 2.19, hence he personifies the next stage in Man's evolution, *Homo erectus.* Shortly thereafter God creates Eve from one of Adam's ribs, hence this represents God operating upon *Homo erectus* to produce *Homo sapiens*, the ancestor of modern Man.

Genesis 2.21 describes the operation: "God caused a deep sleep to fall upon Adam, and he slept." This exactly describes the duties of an anæsthetist before a surgeon performs a major operation. The operation entailed extracting genetic material from Adam, and this is shown by God removing one of Adam's ribs. After the material had been extracted God, like any surgeon who has carried out intrusive surgery, "closed up the flesh."

Part 2

With this operation God succeeded in creating a version of Man that could carry out whatever tasks He had in store for him. These tasks require intellect of a high order, because Man's mind – his seat of learning – has extraordinary properties. Its storage capacity is phenomenal – 100 billion neurons, each capable of storing a mass of information, 100 trillion links between neurons to create billions of databases, each database kept separate and distinct by billions of synaptic gaps.

Only the most modern computers can be compared to the human mind with regard to capacity and data processing. Computers store information in an orderly fashion in databases or files. Each file has a title consisting of figures and/or words. The titles are entered in a directory that arranges them in an orderly manner and gives each of them an address (file path). The appropriate address is added to fresh information ('bytes') so that it is assigned to the correct file. Files therefore have clearly defined pathways, and these allow the operator to access instantly a particular file. The human mind must operate in the same way, because it is the only explanation for our ability to recall instantly a fact or many facts concerning a particular subject.

Scientists who have studied the human mind have failed to see the similarity between its information-processing systems and those of a computer. They have observed that neurons are divided into various categories, because objects that we see, touch, smell, taste, etc. activate different neurons. Having done so once, the objects do so again and again, and scientists believe this is how memories are created.

However, it cannot be as simple as that! A neuron is only activated after a thought travels along the axon leading to it, hence the axon has to have an address, and the address has to contain the name of the neuron (file). Therefore a thought can only register after the human mind has created a file containing a title for this thought.

For example, if someone handles a banana for the first time, thoughts registering our ideas and sensations have nowhere to go because no neuron has information on bananas. To rectify this situation we have to do the same as computer operators: create a file with the name Banana; the file is entered in the directory, which gives it an address (file path), and then our thoughts on bananas proceed along the file path to the file (neuron).

Sometimes the neurons containing thoughts on a particular subject will be scattered throughout our mind, because a subject can have many diverse aspects, but the information they contain will eventually converge on the file path leading to the aspect on which we wish to focus. This explains why we sometimes take time to assemble our facts. The process is the same as a computer operator opening a file and seeing all the information he has acquired on bananas, even though the individual bytes of information are scattered ('fragmented') on the hard disk.

Brain scans show that when we constantly recall certain pieces of information, the links between the relevant neurons become tighter to accelerate recall. This equates to the 'disk defragmenter' programme in computers.

Tightening the links between neurons creates a large database. In computers such databases have sub-files or indices. Those for ChessBase contain indices for games, tournament/matches, players, annotators, openings, etc. These indices correspond to individual neurons that have been tightly linked together to form the large database.

A more graphic illustration of the storage capacity of a neuron is the fact that when we recall an image, such as a person's face, a building, a town we have visited, a landscape, etc., the entire image instantly appears before our eyes, and this is only possible if it was stored on one neuron, yet the same image would occupy far more space on a computer and contain millions of pixels. This shows that the storage capacity of a single neuron is enormous.

Cognitive tests show that in the blink of an eye we only focus on two or three objects, but later, under hypnosis, we recall much else besides. Scientists believe this means our mind operates on the unconscious level, automatically processing everything we see.

*   *   *   *   *   *   *

How do we create a file? This question can be answered by analogy with computers. If we type in the word banana on a blank page in an unnamed file, then before we can switch to another subject we are asked by the Word programme whether or not we wish to save the word banana. If we wish to save it, then we have to send Word a command to that effect by clicking the computer mouse.

The mouse is an electronic device that is handled by the operator and linked to the computer. It is the means by which commands from the operator register with the computer.

We tell Word, via the mouse, that we wish to save banana, and are then told to save it in a file. This entails typing in a filename and then, again by means of the mouse, instructing the computer to save the file. The file is then entered in the directory.

This is another illustration of the fact that, in computing, one cannot create memories until one has created a file in which they can be stored.

The computer mouse creates and saves a new file or opens an existing file. It is the key to entering new information and accessing stored information. The human mind must have the equivalent of the computer mouse, and we believe it is our personality.

Personality determines our thoughts, and these register (as distinct from fleeting or random ideas),[1] because when we have a thought, it is a

1 Fleeting ideas do not register because they lack sufficient intensity of concentration to create a file. In a computer we initially store data in RAM – short-term memory – and this data is immediately erased if we do not save it to a file before we switch to another subject (window). The human mind must have an equivalent of RAM, because this is the only means of explaining why fleeting ideas cannot be recalled after we have concentrated on another subject.

conscious effort equivalent to a computer operator pressing the mouse. When the mouse is pressed, it electronically transmits a command to the computer that either creates a new file or opens an existing file. A thought is an electronic command, and therefore it has the same effect on the files in our mind. Since the origin of the thought is our personality, it equates to the mouse on a computer.

* * * * * * *

Thoughts open a file and therefore thoughts close a file – we switch our thoughts to another subject – but because our mind never stops thinking, it immediately opens another file. No one has been able to explain how this is accomplished. Science assigns the task to the hormone serotonin, which is secreted by the pineal gland. Hormones are the mind's messengers, and serotonin transmits messages in the form of electronic nerve impulses across synapses – the gaps between neurons. The gaps are essential so as to isolate databases, and the action of serotonin is equally essential, because it switches off electronic activity within each database.

Clearly the action of serotonin is only half the story, because thoughts – electronic commands – opened the database and therefore play a part in the procedure for closing it.

Thoughts on the subject (file) created an electronic field that was immediately detected by the pineal. It secreted serotonin to open the file, and when our thoughts turned to another subject – switched off the electronic field – the pineal secreted serotonin to close the file.

The procedure is analogous to that in computers, where one cannot switch to another database until the opened (work) database has been closed.

The procedures for opening and closing a file have to occur almost

---

Likewise our initial thoughts on bananas would have been stored in RAM and then erased if we did not create a file to which they could be assigned.

instantaneously, hence the pineal requires advance notice. For computers, to open a file the operator places the arrow of the mouse on the file's icon and double-clicks the mouse. Our thoughts on a subject equate to pointing an arrow in the direction of the file, and this is sufficient notice for the pineal to secrete serotonin and open it. Our decision (thoughts) to close the file by turning to another subject equate to the operator placing the arrow of the mouse on the 'close' or 'exit' button. But whereas the operator has to double click the mouse in order to exit, the pineal secretes serotonin, because we have given it all the notice that it requires.

*   *   *   *   *   *   *

When we have a thought, but related information stored in our memory does not come to the fore immediately, the reason is that the thought did not contain the key figures and/or words that correspond with the filename. In this case we have found it advisable to run through the letters of the alphabet, as the first letter in the title, coupled with the subject matter contained in our thought, triggers the rest of the key and brings up the file.

A letter of the alphabet would not, by itself, bring up the file because it could apply to any number of files, therefore it is the subject matter together with the appropriate letter that forms the key. This means our directory, like that of a computer, arranges files according to subjects or categories. The same must therefore apply to neurons, and this is why scientists have been able to observe that neurons are divided into subjects or categories.

Sometimes the information does not come to mind because we have not considered the subject for a long time – have not opened the file for a long time. We then turn to another subject, only to have the required information on our original inquiry suddenly pop into our head. The explanation is that the file had been archived and our initial thought instigated a search process that continued as a background task, in the same way that a computer-operated printer will continue to print when the printer icon is minimised and the operator is dealing with another task.

The same process explains our ability to solve complex anagrams. If we cannot deduce the word immediately, because it lacks obvious prefixes or suffixes, then we instigate a search of our memory and concentrate on another subject. A few seconds later the word suddenly comes to mind. The explanation is that the thought (which included all the letters in the anagram) tasked with carrying out the search equated to a command that opened the file containing our vocabulary.[2] The words are displayed in alphabetical order – because that is the natural arrangement – and a thought can scan them as fast as a modern computer. As soon as a word was found that contained all the letters in the anagram, it was flashed to the forefront of our mind.

The same process helps to explain the efficiency of mental reminders – 'flags' that we inserted in files where the coverage was incomplete, in the hope that the missing information would eventually come to light. These reminders have never let us down, yet the standard theory concerning memory does not explain how they operate, let alone how they do so with such efficiency that, even though we may not have considered the subject for years, the reminders operate as soon as the missing information is found.

The explanation is that our initial thoughts had created a file and an instruction stating that we had to recall the file as soon as the missing information was located. The instruction meant the file was not archived. Instead, it was kept in the forefront of our mind but minimised so that we could concentrate on other matters. As soon as the missing information was located, we remembered the title of the file in which it had to be inserted. The file was then maximised in the forefront of our mind and we could begin the process of updating it.

2 The vocabulary file is our dictionary, so we may assume that it also contains the meanings of words. This would explain why we immediately know when someone has used the wrong word.

The shut down procedure in a computer transfers new information that we have entered on the Visual Display Unit (VDU) to the hard disk. The information is added to existing files and, if new files have been created, the directory is amended accordingly. The human mind must be capable of carrying out the same procedure. We believe it does so when we are asleep, for this is when our conscious mind ceases to transmit thoughts, but our brain never switches off.

Part 3

God requires Man to be not only highly intelligent but also aware of his obligations to Him. Man therefore has to be God-conscious and spiritual, hence God had to perform operations that produced both physiological improvements and a spiritual sense.

Both requirements are met in the difference between Man and other creatures with regard to the positioning and functioning of the pineal gland.

In birds and animals whose cerebrum – the top part of the brain – is small or non-existent, the pineal gland lies immediately under the skull, but in Man the cerebrum is huge, and the pineal gland is in the centre of the brain. It is a tiny grey mass, no more than a quarter of an inch in length and weighing one-thirtieth of an ounce.

The pineal gland was originally an eye. The Tuatara lizard of New Zealand has a cleft in the centre of its skull, with a transparent membrane around which the scales are arranged in a rosette. Under this is a vestigial eye, complete with a pigmented retina and a type of lens. However, it lacks connecting nerves and seems to serve no purpose, but in 1958 two zoologists from the University of California discovered that the removal of the gland made the escape reactions of lizards much slower, so it must be sensitive to light and aid survival.

In birds and animals the pineal is sensitive to light. This enables it to function as a regulator of biological rhythms that are affected by light and dark, day and night. It does so by secreting a hormone called melatonin. In birds and mammals melatonin influences sleep periods and changes in body temperatures, but its influence may also extend to the timing of annual events, such as hibernation and migration.

In those creatures where the pineal is situated at or near the surface of the skull, it has no difficulty in carrying out its function, but in advanced creatures such as mammals it is positioned deep within the brain, and cannot see the light. It therefore requires a 24-hour 'clock'.

The mechanism consists of light entering the eye and stimulating the retina. This causes impulses to be transmitted along the optic nerve into the sympathetic nervous system and the pineal. The nerve impulses inhibit the activity of serotonin, which is necessary to produce melatonin. Conversely, during the hours of darkness, when there is no inhibitor on serotonin, melatonin can be produced and secreted.

However, this mechanism is not sufficient to regulate Man's daily rhythms because his level of intelligence enables him to override markers for waking and sleeping such as light and darkness. Despite this, the pineal gland is situated at the centre of Man's brain, and this is because, as we showed in Part 2, it assists higher mental processes.

In Man the pineal contains a dozen substances, including the hormones melatonin and serotonin. The latter is a regulatory agent. It transmits impulses across synapses that ensure neurons – cells containing data, memories, etc. – are opened and closed in an orderly manner. Regulating the secretion of serotonin is essential – schizophrenics have far less serotonin in their brains than normal – and this is one of the functions of the pineal. Regulating the production of serotonin enables the pineal to do the same for melatonin, because the latter is manufactured by the action of a hormone on serotonin.

These tasks could not have been carried out by earlier versions of the pineal due to the much greater complexity of Man's brain, but the latest research shows that the pineal assists the intellect in an even more profound way.

Recent brain scans have shown that the pineal helps to regulate sleep patterns and is activated when people meditate. Dr. Jyh-Horng Chen, co-leader of the study, said: "There is no definition of 'soul' in the scientific field, but our results demonstrate a correlation between pineal activation and religious meditation which might have profound implications in the physiological understanding of mind, spirit and soul."

Dr. Chen and colleagues at the National Taiwan University scanned the brains of eleven men and nine women as they meditated. Their pineal areas were most active in the first phase, when practitioners try to get themselves into the right frame of mind.

Dr. Chen, whose findings were published online in December 2007 by *Nature Proceedings*, said that the pineal gland could play a rôle in the "intrinsic awareness" of spirituality.

This is not a new idea. As long ago as the fourth century B.C., Herophilus described the pineal as the organ that regulates the flow of thought, whilst Descartes believed it was the point at which the mind and body are joined together (it has always intrigued anatomists that, while the rest of the brain is 'double', the pineal has no duplicate).

The difference between the function of the pineal as a 'third eye' in birds and mammals,[3] owing to its sensitivity to light, and its function as a spiritual centre in Man is a quantum leap that natural evolution would never have accomplished, and proves God genetically modified the pineal and the entire human brain.

---

3 The description of the pineal as a 'third eye' calls to mind a strand of Hindu mythology that says each man possesses a 'third eye' to form a channel for his occult powers. It is his spiritual centre, and this connects with the ideas of Herophilus and Descartes cited earlier. It should also be noted that the figs of the *Ficus religiosa*, or Bo tree, under which the Buddha is traditionally supposed to have sat, have the highest serotonin level of all fruit.

Primates have the highest serotonin level amongst creatures, which explains why they, in common with Man, have late sexual development – further proof that Man was genetically engineered from a species of primate.

Chapter Two
God Creates Man's Environment

Part 1

We have reconciled the Darwinian theory of evolution – Man is descended from the primates – with God creating Man "from the dust of the earth," but that is only the beginning, because the order in which God created other creatures and the environment exactly matches the science. Plants appear on dry land before animals, and fish appear in the sea before animals on dry land. Moses, the author of Genesis, would have been completely unaware that fossil records bear out this sequence, hence he could only have obtained this information from one source: the Creator Himself.

God must therefore have controlled the evolution of life, and the means by which He did so is given in the original text of Genesis.

Genesis 1.21,24 says "God created every living creature," the word "creature" being derived from the Hebrew "nephesh," which means soul. In this context, soul implies self-conscious life – awareness of one's existence and surroundings.

Souls are by their very nature intangible – not composed of flesh and blood – and therefore are God's creations. Souls are the life-force inside every living thing, and since every living thing acts and reacts instinctively – automatically – they must be obeying instructions from their souls.

This means souls have programmes. They are God's equivalent of silicon chips in computers.

* * * * * * *

The necessity for God to install a component with computer-like qualities becomes clear when we consider the nature of the evolutionary process. It entails making choices, and each choice has its pros and cons. These have to be carefully assessed, and this calls for rational analysis and lengthy calculation.

Evolution also requires imagination, because it is necessary to conceive the final form before calculation can begin, therefore the soul has to be highly intelligent.

The entire process has to be co-ordinated. Information regarding the environment has to be gathered and stored alongside data showing the layout of the creature. This enables the soul to determine the parameters within which it can evolve, and draw up a template. The soul therefore equates to the central processing unit within a computer.

Once the soul has determined the form into which its host must evolve, it can instigate the necessary changes. These consist principally of alterations to the genetic code (DNA) by rearranging, modifying or switching off sets of genes.

In single-celled organisms the DNA in only one cell has to be altered, and so evolution can begin immediately. Since these organisms are the basis for more advanced forms of life, and are regulated by programmes in the soul that He had written, God could control evolution.

* * * * * * *

Once we recognise that every living thing has a soul, we can understand how the earliest bacteria – minute single-celled organisms with no definable nucleus or 'brain centre' – helped to create Earth's atmosphere through a complex and sophisticated process called photosynthesis, and then evolve a more efficient way of doing so.

Photosynthesis converts sunlight into energy. It does so by means of a long chain of chemical reactions that convert carbon dioxide into water. The carbon dioxide is taken from the air, and oxygen is released. Carbon dioxide is a poisonous gas, whilst oxygen is essential for life. Photosynthesis therefore maintains the correct proportion of oxygen in the atmosphere, and is the key to life on Earth.

The first stage in photosynthesis is the absorption of sunlight by chlorophyll, but the earliest form of bacteria had to use retinal (a form of Vitamin A). Retinal is a simpler substance than chlorophyll, and was easier to produce in the low-oxygen environment that existed on Earth at the time. However, retinal only absorbs green light and reflects back red and violet, hence bacteria evolved that could use chlorophyll to absorb the red and blue wavelengths retinal did not use. In the end, the more efficient chlorophyll-using bacteria prevailed, and this explains why plants are green, not purple.

* * * * * * *

God had to operate on a global scale, therefore souls contained programmes that enabled organisms to co-operate on a global scale. The earliest forms of bacteria could not create a breathable atmosphere because they had no internal processes that resulted in the exhalation of oxygen. The process requires chlorophyll, which was only present in blue-green algæ, hence bacteria could only obtain chlorophyll by absorbing the decaying remains of the algæ. This necessitated the two organisms living together.

Bacteria and blue-green algæ have been found growing together in the hot springs of Yellowstone in North America, and this has convinced scientists that they would have grown together when the surface of Earth was a vast volcanic region.

Bacteria helped to create Earth's atmosphere by photosynthesis, but switched off when algæ evolved that could supply all the oxygen that was required.

Bacteria and algæ extract carbon dioxide from the atmosphere during photosynthesis, but since life on Earth is carbon-based, the carbon dioxide has to be replaced. Plants evolved from bacteria and algæ with a programme called respiration that replaces the carbon dioxide.

Respiration is as complex as photosynthesis. Using oxygen from the air, sugar is chemically broken down by enzymes, which releases carbon dioxide, water and energy.

During photosynthesis and respiration, oxygen, carbon dioxide and other gases such as nitrogen are continually being taken in and released. Carbon dioxide is also released when plants and animals die, because bacteria break down the carbohydrates into carbon dioxide and water. These processes maintain the balance of gases in the atmosphere that is essential for life.

* * * * * * *

These examples show that God controlled evolution and shaped the environment with mathematical accuracy, but instigating the process on a worldwide basis created incalculable possibilities, and sometimes He had to take corrective action. This explains why evolution is punctuated by periodic mass extinctions.

Proof that God engineered these extinctions is the fact that they fitted in perfectly with His plan. His ultimate aim was to install Man on Earth, and each extinction removed species whose continued existence would have wiped out the creatures from which Man is descended.

Two mass extinctions stand out. The first occurred 250 million years ago, and destroyed 95% of species. This enabled the remainder to flourish, and they included the sinodons. These pig-like creatures burrowed underground, surviving on tubers and roots. They became the dominant species, and one of them eventually evolved into a mammal.

From the mammals evolved primates, and Man is descended from the primates.

The second mass extinction occurred 65 million years ago, and it ended the reign of the dinosaurs ('terrible lizards'). They had ruled Earth for nearly 150 million years, and had become so well adapted that they had nothing to fear from their surroundings. However, their continued existence would have been inimical to the mammals that God had recently introduced, and a host of factors suddenly conspired to bring the reign of the dinosaurs to an abrupt end.

Earth's landscape changed. The continents, which tectonic plate movements had brought together millions of years earlier to form the super-continent of Pangaea, became separated by another series of plate movements. The sea rushed in to fill the gaps. As the sea level rose, it flooded much of the low-lying land where dinosaurs lived. Instead of being warm all the time, the climate became more variable or seasonal. This affected the sea, and vast stretches became warmer than others. Creatures living in the sea that could not adapt were doomed, and many groups of sea animals became extinct.

The types of plant also changed. Flowering plants became increasingly important. As the flora began to change, creatures that fed on it had to change. Warm-blooded animals such as mammals became more numerous, but were attacked and devoured by dinosaurs that had specially evolved to catch mammals and insects. These coelurosaurs, or 'hollow-tailed lizards', were lightly built and could run very fast. They had long, grasping arms and hands, as well as long, narrow jaws, and were ideally suited for catching their prey.

Man is descended from mammals, therefore a threat to mammals was a threat to God's plan to place Man on Earth. The coelurosaurs were themselves vulnerable to attack from larger flesh-eating dinosaurs, especially the fiercest of them all, *Tyrannosaurus Rex*. This was too big a threat to God's plan! The dinosaurs had to go, and they had to go quickly.

* * * * * * *

One reason for the extinction of the dinosaurs was the dominance of flowering plants, because they were a type of plant dinosaurs could not eat. Since it was God's wish to end the reign of dinosaurs, He must have planned the appearance of flowers.

Flowers first appeared at the beginning of the Jurassic period, about 160 million years ago, when dinosaurs ruled Earth. At the end of this period, 65 million years ago, the dinosaurs were extinct and flowers had developed into forms that were ideal for mammals.

These developments were not coincidental because at the same time as flowers were evolving to benefit mammals, primates made their first appearance. Primates feed on the leaves, blossoms, buds and fruits of flowers, Man is descended from a species of primate, and God's ultimate aim was to install Man.

* * * * * * *

Birds appeared after the extinction of the dinosaurs and are one of the final ingredients for Man's environment. Many types of birds form part of Man's diet, but they are indispensable in other ways. They eat insects and other invertebrates whose population would otherwise be uncontrollable. Where birds exist near water, they eat certain types of fish, which helps to keep their numbers under control. They are also one of the principal means by which plants disperse their seeds.

Scientists believe there is a direct link between birds and dinosaurs, because certain of the latter had learnt to fly. The best known of these is *Archæopteryx*, which lived 150 million years ago. It had feathers on the wing and tail, like all birds, but it also had many dinosaurian features, such as bones in the tail and, in its long slim jaws, small teeth. It also had claws on its wings, suggesting it evolved from meat-eating dinosaurs that had slight, clawed forearms.

Archæopteryx had a short body but long legs, to support feathery wings. However, analysis of its skeleton suggests that it ran like meat-eating dinosaurs, with only short burst of flight to catch insects. Compare this with the annual migrations made by birds!

Another well-known dinosaur that learned to fly was *Pterodactyl.* It was the largest member of the pterosaurs, which were flying reptiles. They were an advance on *Archaeopteryx* inasmuch as they could fly over vast distances, but they had no feathers, and were therefore quite unlike birds today.

For these reasons, we do not believe birds evolved from flying dinosaurs. God timed the introduction of birds when pterosaurs no longer constituted a threat to their survival and He was finalising the list of essential items in Man's environment.

Genesis 1.21 supports our theory, because it says God created birds ("winged fowls") at the same time as he created mammals such as whales, and these appeared, according to Genesis 1.24, shortly before God created the animals we see around us today.

* * * * * * *

Whales, dolphins and porpoises evolved from reptiles that decided to go back to the sea. They had no compelling reason for doing so, and their souls were programmed with self-consciousness, which enabled them to consider becoming stronger, faster and taller than their rivals. The hippopotamus – the nearest relative of the whale – opted for the first of these possibilities, and survives perfectly well on land.

The decision by these reptiles to go down this evolutionary part must have followed an instruction from their souls, and indeed it fits in perfectly with God's plan. Mammals are at the head of the food-chain that keeps fish populations under control.

The earliest members of the horse, camel and elephant families appeared shortly afterwards, to be followed by cloven-hoofed animals and carnivores. The last were essential, as the population of herbivores would otherwise have been uncontrollable.

* * * * * * *

It is clear that evolution followed a predetermined course. Whenever environments hostile to Man's antecedents arose, they were eliminated.

Each stage was a natural progression. Organisms, insects and plants preceded creatures such as fish and animals that have souls of a higher calibre. The souls in these creatures have self-consciousness – awareness of their own existence and that of other members of their species. They are also aware of other species and can interact with them.

This accounts for the teamwork displayed by dolphins, sharks and gannets when attacking shoals of sardine off the Cape of South Africa; by dolphins and gannets when attacking shoals of sardine off the coast of New Zealand; and by dolphins and sheerwaters when attacking shoals of mackerel off the same coast.

Animals likewise have self-conscious souls, hence we see displays of teamwork. Lions hunt in packs and, by dint of carefully thought-out plans, isolate their prey and bring it down. Chimpanzees apply the same strategy. Many creatures rely on the cries of birds high up in trees to warn them of nearby predators.

In each case the balance of Nature is not disturbed, because creatures are programmed only to kill what they need, and to leave their prey with sufficient breeding stock that they will return in the same numbers next year. This is typical of the mathematical precision that governs God's thinking.

God applied the same degree of precision to the programmes that govern the manner in which land animals evolve. It can be expressed by the following equation: if an animal decides that its best chance of survival is to be the strongest, then its muscle bulk will reduce its speed; if an animal decides to be the fastest, then it will have to reduce its muscle bulk, leaving it weaker than bulkier rivals.

This equation is played out by the predators that roam the plains of

Africa. The lion is the strongest, but the cheetah is the fastest. However, the cheetah has to abandon its prey if a lion approaches, because it would have no chance in a fight. The leopard is faster than the lion and stronger than the cheetah; moreover, it has evolved a way of retaining its prey when a lion approaches, for it can climb trees with prey clamped in its jaws. But if no tree is nearby, the leopard, like the cheetah, has to abandon its prey to the lion.

Scavengers are creatures that take advantage of predators by eating the remains of their kills. Vultures can swiftly swoop on the remains, and hyenas have such powerful jaws and teeth that they can crush bones and extract bone marrow. But if a lion, leopard or cheetah approaches, the scavengers have to flee.

* * * * * * *

With birds in the sky, fish in the sea, animals on land that was covered in plants, trees, vegetation, and flowers, providing the perfect habitat for primates, God had furnished Man with everything he would need from the natural environment. All He now had to do was create Man.

Chapter Three
God Designs Earth

Part 1

Genesis states that God created Earth but at its inception Earth "was without form and void." This meant God had to fashion it into a planet capable of supporting life, and the more one examines Earth's structure, the more one sees it was designed for our benefit.

During its formative stage Earth suffered a series of collisions, but their overall effect was to change its structure into one that could support life.

When Earth was molten, it collided with a solid iron object, and the force of this collision was so great that it drove the object into Earth's core. Molten iron moving around the solid iron core created a magnetic field, and this prevented Earth from being scorched by charged particles streaming from the Sun. Given that the ultimate aim of all these structural changes was to provide a suitable environment for Man, it is inconceivable that the collision that gave rise to this field was accidental.

Other features of the core prove it was designed to perfection. The molten mass is 1,300 miles thick, which is sufficient to generate a magnetic field strong enough to withstand the force of solar winds. The field only bends under the impact of these winds, and deflects the charged particles to the poles and into space. Meanwhile the tension created by the bending and stretching of the field is released when the field re-enters Earth at the north magnetic pole. The field is thus able to absorb high impacts and regain its original configuration.

The mathematical exactness of these features proves God designed Earth. It also validates the verses in Jeremiah 4.23-26 and Isaiah 24.1 that suggest primordial Earth suffered a catastrophe (or series of catastrophes) as a result of divine judgement.

For life to exist, it has to have a breathable atmosphere. The latest theory to account for Earth's atmosphere is that a 'twin' planet – Thea – orbited so close to Earth that they collided. Earth was molten and absorbed Thea. This increased its gravitational pull to such an extent that it was able to retain an atmosphere when it began to form.

Scientists regard this collision as coincidental, but we consider it to be no more coincidental than the collision that created Earth's molten core and the resultant magnetic field, especially as the field helps to prevent the atmosphere from drifting away by securing the uppermost layer. It was a vital link in the chain of events that created the proper environment for Man, and could not have happened naturally. Our neighbouring planet Mars, for example, had no such collision, its diameter remained half the size of Earth's, and so its atmosphere gradually drifted into space.[4]

Part 2

Our planet has a satellite, the Moon, situated at the exact mathematical point where it affects the tides of the sea for our benefit, and periodically totally eclipses the Sun. The latest theory concerning the origin of the

4 Mars, being only half the size of Earth, had a core that was too small to generate a magnetic field strong enough to withstand solar winds. This exposed its atmosphere to the full force and heat of solar particles, so much of it was burned off.

Moon is that it was formed from material hurled into space following the collision with Thea. The material would not have escaped Earth's gravity, for this had been greatly increased by the absorption of Thea, and it would have gradually coalesced. Analysis of rock samples taken from the Moon show they are 4.6 billion years ago, which corresponds to the time when Thea is believed to have collided with Earth.

The distance of the Moon from Earth is 240,000 miles, which is the mathematically exact point at which its gravitational force is most beneficial for Man. If the Moon were 20 times closer, it would exert a gravitational force 400 times greater. Much land would be flooded and many cities would be drowned. If the Moon were further away, Earth would slow down. Days would be longer in some parts of the world and nights would be longer in others. Our calendar year and seasons would be in disarray.

The collision theory fits in with our theory that the programmes allowed such impacts when they contributed to life on Earth, and the Moon assists life in various ways. Its magnetic field, though weak, is sufficiently strong to interact with that of Earth's and be picked up by magnetic sensors in animals, allowing them to refine their migratory/homing instincts and hunting skills. The Moon's gravitational pull, also very weak in comparison with that of Earth's, is nevertheless strong enough to create tides. These can be predicted, owing to the regularity of the Moon's orbit, which is an invaluable aid to shipping and other activities.

Some species of coral synchronise their life cycle so that they reproduce on the night of a full moon. Every 29 days they form new scales, and these constitute a means of measuring the length of a day/year. The fossilised remains of coral enable us to measure the length of a day/year millions of years ago, and analysis shows that, 400 million years ago, there were 400 days in a year, and a day lasted 21 hours 55 minutes. The length of a day is the time it takes Earth to rotate once on its axis, consequently Earth was spinning much faster than it does today.

The Moon played a vital part in slowing down Earth's rate of spin, because initially it was much closer to Earth, its gravitational force had a much greater effect, and it spun more slowly. These factors acted as a brake, consequently we owe our 24-hour day and seasons of the year to the Moon!

As Earth slowed down, the Moon orbited faster because of a fundamental law of physics that states for every action there is an equal and opposite reaction. The laws of physics derive, as we show in a later chapter, from commands written by God, hence He deliberately increased speed of the Moon so as to force it further away from Earth and into its present orbit/distance, where it is of maximum benefit to us.

Part 4

Every aspect of Earth's formation testifies to God's unerring powers of calculation, and the same applies to Earth's features. Earth is tilted at an angle of 23° 26′ 59″ to the plane of its orbit. This is the mathematically exact angle for sustaining life on Earth, because it creates the seasons.[5] The seasons themselves are defined by a combination of mathematics and astronomy. Four points, the two equinoxes and the two solstices, divide the ecliptic (the path of the Sun) into 90° sections, and the period occupied by the Sun in each of these sections constitutes one season.

Earth's tilt is unique in the Solar System. Mercury is so close to the Sun that it tilts towards it at an angle of 2°, and Venus only tilts away from the Sun at 3°. The tilt of Mars is an Earth-like 24° but, being

5 Proof that God devised the seasons is given in Genesis 1.14: "And God said, Let there be lights [Sun and Moon] in the firmament of heaven to divide the day from night; and let them be for seasons, days and years."

almost twice as distant from the Sun, its seasons, though similar to ours, are almost twice as long. This would give us too much sunlight in spring/summer, and be too cold for us in winter.

Without Earth's tilt life could not survive, yet scientists cannot account for it. However, every planet in the Solar System is tilted on its axis, usually as a result of a collision with another object during their formative stages, hence the same must have occurred to Earth. Possibly the tilt was another effect of its collision with Thea, for we have shown convincingly that it was not a chance occurrence.

Thea may have created Earth's tilt but the Moon most certainly preserves it. The Moon orbits at the exact distance that compels Earth to rotate at the speed necessary to maintain the correct angle. If the Moon were further way, Earth would slow down and lose stability. It would start to wobble and eventually tip on its side.

The Moon maintains Earth's balance with mathematical accuracy, and the same degree of accuracy applies to Earth's structure. Ice ages enormously increase the weight of material on the crust, but underneath is a layer of warm, viscous material that flows, causing the overlying crust in another region to rise. Thus for every part of the planet weighed down by ice, there is a corresponding uplift elsewhere. This process is termed Isostasy.

Earth's crust has many fault-lines, and these divide the surface into tectonic plates. When magma from the molten core rises through a fault-line, it exerts pressure on the adjoining plates. The plate with lighter material is forced upwards and over the plate with heavier material. The latter is forced downwards and into the warm viscous material under the crust, where it is absorbed. The process is termed subduction, and it is an essential safety-valve. For every increase in material (magma) brought to the surface, there is a corresponding loss of material to the interior; for every increase in pressure by rising magma, there is a means of distributing that pressure elsewhere.

Without the safety-valve of subduction, Earth would be wracked by earthquakes whose destructive force would make life impossible. The seas and oceans also act as safety-valves, for they separate the land-masses and absorb the shock-waves generated by earthquakes. This ensures earthquakes only last a few seconds, whereas on Mars the absence of liquefied water means earthquakes last for several hours, because the rocks constantly rub up against each other.

About 120 million years ago movements of the tectonic plates caused the super-continent of Pangaea to break up. Two enormous land masses moved west and today comprise North and South America, whilst two others moved east to form India and Australia; meanwhile other land masses moved north and grouped themselves around the Artic circle. These movements caused Earth to become top heavy, and so an equally great land mass had to assemble around the southern polar region. In due course a region of Pangaea moved south to form Antarctica, which provided the perfect counterweight.

Movements of the tectonic plates, together with the process of subduction, are essential for maintaining a balance on the surface, and they are unique to Earth. They only occur because the core is sufficiently large that it can generate heat and rising magma for billions of years.

However, this does not explain why the plates have been in perpetual motion, because a fundamental law of physics states that heat is always lost to cooler surroundings, hence heat generated internally by a planet always finds its way to the surface and is then lost to space. Therefore Earth would quickly have lost its heat, and plate movements would have ceased, but for the fact that Earth is situated in the only region of the Solar System where the surroundings are not too cold, and its mass creates the right amount of gravity. These factors ensure that heat only escapes very slowly, allowing continuous plate movements.

This shows that God had to situate Earth exactly where it is in the Solar System. Mars, for example, is much further away from the Sun, its surroundings are much colder, and it loses heat much more quickly.

Mars could not prevent this because it is much smaller than Earth, and lacks sufficient gravity.

Tectonic plate movements not only maintain a balance on the surface but also give rise to volcanic activity, a vital factor in creating the conditions for life. Volcanic eruptions permit gases and other substances buried deep within Earth to reach the surface and the atmosphere. These substances include water, which is essential for life. Scientists estimate that much of the water on Earth's surface originated from chambers deep within Earth's mantle, and was propelled into the atmosphere by volcanic eruptions. Without these eruptions, water would have remained trapped and buried inside Earth.

Water consists of two-thirds hydrogen to one-third oxygen. When combined with poisonous gases emitted into the atmosphere from other volcanoes, it forms the combination of gases that constitute a breathable atmosphere. Water falls as rain, which is one of the elements that sculpts and cleanses the surface.

Earth still has numerous active volcanoes – living testimonies to the longevity of its power to generate and retain heat. The core in Mars is only half the size of Earth's and quickly lost the power to generate heat, leading to a cessation of volcanic activity. Coupled with the inability of Mars to retain its atmosphere, the consequence was that Mars could not retain water, lacked rainfall, and the features on its surface could not be eroded.

The surface of Mars shows the dire consequences of being unable to erode features that arise at an early stage of formation. One canyon is so huge that the Grand Canyon in Arizona could fit into a side valley!

This canyon is called Vallis Marineris. It is 5 miles deep and 3,000 miles long – the distance between Los Angeles and New York. If such a feature existed today in the USA or anywhere else, it would have a ruinous effect on Man's progress, but a never-ending supply of water in the form of rainfall and rivers has eroded all features of Earth's primordial past.

* * * * * * *

Another example showing how the absence of the balancing factors on Earth affects a planet is the fate that has befallen Venus.

Venus is similar to Earth both in density and size, but is closer to Sun and its surface is too hot to permit water to exist in liquefied form. Furthermore, its core is completely different from that of Earth's, because it does not generate a magnetic field. As a result, the atmosphere on Venus was vulnerable to attack from solar winds.

The atmosphere was formed after volcanic eruptions hurled skywards various gases and water. Solar winds heated the water molecules, causing them to move faster (heat = energy) and further into space. Lacking the magnetic shield that protects and helps to retain Earth's atmosphere, Venus had to rely on its gravitational pull alone, but this was insufficient. The constituents of water – hydrogen and oxygen – separated, the former, being the lighter, drifting into space and oxygen combining with carbon to form carbon dioxide. This became the principal gas in the atmosphere.

Carbon dioxide is a 'greenhouse gas' because it absorbs heat from the surface and causes the temperatures of both the atmosphere and the surface to rise alarmingly. As more carbon dioxide is pumped into the atmosphere by volcanic action, the temperature rises still further, the atmosphere becomes denser, and the temperature rises again. The dreadful effects of this chain reaction are apparent on Venus, where temperature readings of the surface average 480° centigrade – the hottest planetary surface in the Solar System.

On Earth the magnetic field was strong enough to protect the atmosphere from solar winds, and this enabled it to retain water. Water combines with carbon dioxide, therefore water falling to the surface as rain contains dissolved carbon dioxide. The combination of water and carbon dioxide creates carbonic acid, which attacks various elements abundant in rocks. In doing so it becomes locked up in carbonate rocks, and this ensures much carbon dioxide never returns to the atmosphere, where it would reach dangerously high levels.

Part 5

Water is the main element on Earth, and it possesses a number of unique properties that are vital for life. It is the only substance that exists naturally in liquid, solid and gaseous form. This is only made possible by Earth's atmosphere which, uniquely in the Solar System, protects the surface from scorching solar winds and provides the ideal temperature for water and life.

Water also has unique chemical and physical properties. Without any change to itself, it easily dissolves mineral salts, enabling organisms to absorb nutrients, and this is vital for biological functions. Water also has a surprisingly high boiling point, and increases its volume by as much as 11% when it freezes. This lowers its density below that of liquid water, which explains why ice floats.

Water also has unique thermal properties. As the temperature of each gram of water goes down to 0° centigrade, and the water freezes, 79 calories of heat – the heat of fusion – are released. When steam condenses into water, each gram releases 540 calories of heat, which can be used in heating systems. A high heat capacity enables water to absorb a large amount of heat without changing temperature. This is why the temperature of large bodies of water does not fluctuate widely, thereby helping to moderate some local climates.

Water molecules adhere to each other (cohesion) by 'hydrogen bonding', the attachment of the oxygen atom of one water molecule to the hydrogen of another molecule. They also adhere to other hydrogen- and oxygen-containing compounds (adhesion). The strength of these hydrogen bonds gives water its unique properties. Both cohesion and adhesion enable water to defy gravity and climb upward through fine pores by capillary action.

Given its unique qualities, water must be a substance that God created to sustain life on Earth, and this explains why no other planet in the Solar System has such an abundance of water in liquefied form.

* * * * * * *

Earth had to be fashioned into a planet capable of supporting life by countless processes lasting millions of years. It is illogical to believe that these processes achieved the only design that supports life on Earth purely by chance. Everything had to be co-ordinated, and this required extraordinary judgement, planning and foresight.

This is implicit in the quote from Genesis at the beginning of this chapter. Or, to quote from Isaiah 45.18: "For thus saith the Lord that created the heavens, God himself formed the earth and made it; he established it, he created it not in vain, he formed it to be inhabited."

Chapter Four
God Designs The Solar System

Part 1

The processes that transformed Earth into a planet capable of supporting life lasted millions of years, but they would have achieved nothing had not God designed the Solar System through processes lasting billions of years.

The manner in which the Solar System was born testifies to His handiwork. At its centre is the Sun. It was formed 4.57 billion years ago from the collapse of a giant molecular cloud consisting mostly of hydrogen and helium. Similar collapses had created binary stars, but the molecular cloud in which our Sun was created only had sufficient mass to produce one star together with planetary and other objects. Since God had to install Man on a planet, this must have been deliberate.

Likewise God must have carefully calculated the power output of the Sun because it is perfect for Man. If its output were to change by only 0.5%, it would drastically affect our weather, and a drop of less than 2% would turn Earth into an ice-covered planet.

The Sun's power is expressed by its luminosity, which gives a surface temperature of approximately 6,000° Centigrade. Other stars in our galaxy are either too hot – surface temperatures up to 30,000° – or too cold – surface temperatures down to 2,000°. Some stars have masses fifty times as great as the Sun, and shine too brightly – 100,000 times brighter – others are lightweights, and shine too faintly. Nuclear reactions in the Sun cause it to lose 4.5 million tons of matter per second, but it has sufficient mass to burn for billions of years – long enough for life to evolve – whereas larger stars burn away too quickly.

After the Sun burst into life, it began to rotate on its axis, which forced the surrounding gas and dust to orbit in the same direction. The gas began to condense around dust particles, and eventually these condensations formed nine large planets, some fifty satellites, at least three systems of rings, and innumerable smaller bodies concentrated in two main groups: the asteroids and comets. Thus the Solar System was born.

Proof that the creation of the Solar System was God's handiwork is the fact that every single object – including the asteroids and comets – played a part in the evolution of life on Earth. Indeed, the more one studies the layout of the Solar System, the more one sees it was tailor-made to allow life to evolve on Earth.

Everything fits perfectly. Earth is situated in the only region of the Solar System that is neither too warm nor too cold to support life. It is warm enough to allow water to liquefy – vital for life – whereas Mars is too cold – its water has frozen – and Venus is too warm.

Earth orbits at exactly the right distance to derive maximum benefit from the heat of the Sun. Its average distance is 93 million miles, varying by about 3 million miles – sufficient to assist life by creating the seasons, too small to have a damaging effect on the environment. If the distance had been greater, Earth would have suffered a permanent ice age; if smaller, a blazing hot greenhouse effect. The latter is the fate that has befallen Venus, which is only 67 million miles from the Sun.

Given that God's ultimate aim was to install Man on Earth, we can now account for the most remarkable aspect of Solar System's design:

it practically rules out the danger of Earth colliding with other large objects.

Jupiter acts as a shield to protect Earth. Jupiter is the largest planet in the Solar System – 318 times more massive than Earth – and its immense gravitational pull attracts these objects before they reach us. As extra insurance, Earth's satellite, the Moon, performs the same rôle. Its surface is covered by craters created by the impact of meteorites that otherwise would have crashed into Earth.

Nevertheless scientists believe there are hidden dangers to Man within the Solar System.

Orbiting between Mars and Jupiter are thousands of asteroids – rocky débris left over after the formation of Mercury, Venus, Mars and Earth. The asteroids spin on their axes, which counterbalances the immense gravitational force of Jupiter, but scientists have calculated that Jupiter can change the inclination of small asteroids and throw them out of their original paths. When an asteroid is thus ejected, its orbit becomes elliptical, bringing it closer to Earth. Eventually, scientists calculate, the asteroid will collide with Earth, drawn by its gravitational pull. Such a collision could wipe out Man.

We discount this possibility because there is evidence to show that God knew perfectly well how to manipulate the complex gravitational forces besetting the asteroid belt for the benefit of Man. The evidence – a belt of iridium across every continent that was laid down 65 million years ago – proves that an asteroid collided with Earth and wiped out the dinosaurs. This was a crucial step along the path leading to the introduction of Man, and could not have occurred by chance.

Scientists also believe there are dangers to Man far beyond our galaxy, in the form of gamma ray bursts caused by the collision of superdense stars. Collisions of this type produce more energy in ten seconds than the Sun will produce in its entire ten billion-year lifetime, and scientists believe one such burst caused the mass extinction 250 million years ago.

We discount this type of danger because palæontologists have proved that global warming brought about the mass extinction, and it must have been engineered by God because the extinction fitted in perfectly with His plan to install Man on Earth. Furthermore, God ensured that gamma rays are no threat to life because they are readily absorbed by the atmosphere.

The Sun produces gamma rays during its production of nuclear energy, but since the Sun was designed to provide the energy that we need – our climate, fuel and food derive from the power of the Sun – God designed Earth to cope with its output.

Most of the Sun's energy that reaches Earth is absorbed by the atmosphere and the rocks/water on the surface. The consequent warming radiates energy and creates a balance between the solar energy received, the heating of the surface/atmosphere, and the radiation back to space of heat and energy. This proves God calculated the Earth-Sun relationship with mathematical precision.

Scientists also believe there is a long-term threat to Man within our galaxy. Every 150-200 million years Earth (and, of course, the rest of the Solar System) passes through one of its spiral arms. In these regions there is a very much higher concentration of cosmic débris than between the arms, therefore at these times Earth can expect to suffer extensive meteoritic bombardment. If a very large body hit Earth, then the impact would throw up a column of debris that would stay in the atmosphere for a considerable length of time. This layer of drifting débris would block much of the Sun's light and heat, cause temperatures to plummet, and lead to the extinction of many species, possibly including Man.

However, God clearly designed the Solar System in such a way that it prevented impacts that would have a devastating effect on Man, and the proof lies in the fact that the impacts Earth has actually suffered made significant contributions to life.

Scientists now believe half the water in the oceans was due to the impacts of comets, because they contain vast quantities of frozen water that would liquefy on contact with Earth's surface. Recently, a rocket was sent to collide with a comet that was passing by, and the resulting spray was calculated to contain 250 million litres of water.

Scientists also believe certain asteroids carried out the same task. Instrument readings show that asteroids such as Elst Pizarro and RE-700, have a tail whose composition is identical to those found in comets. The tails of comets are created by the vaporisation of ice in the head of the comet as it nears the Sun, hence the tails of comets consist of ice particles and the same must apply to the tails of these asteroids. Since asteroids can be drawn into a collision course with Earth, scientists believe that ice-laden asteroids collided with Earth during its formative stage, when the surface was molten and unable to create water, and these collisions helped to create seas and oceans.

The impact of asteroids assisted life in other ways. A recent study of rocks from the Baltic region concluded that the impact of fragmented asteroids, approximately 470 million years ago, accelerated the development of life on Earth by creating more varied environmental conditions and a subsequent spurt in new species.

These examples are further proof that the asteroid belt was a vital part of God's design of the Solar System, and that He knew perfectly well how to manipulate it to assist life on Earth.

Part 2

Our survey shows that God situated Earth perfectly and ensured it would only receive impacts that assisted natural evolution. The same can therefore be said of the impact that increased Earth's original mass to a point at which its gravitational strength could retain an atmosphere, the basis for life.

For Earth to be inhabitable God had to create the right atmosphere – a mixture of certain gases, mainly nitrogen and oxygen, in the correct proportions – but during the early stages of Earth's formation, huge volcanoes covered the entire surface and were constantly erupting, emitting carbon dioxide, sulphur and other gases that Man could not breathe.

These eruptions resulted from convection currents deep within Earth that forced magma through fissures to the surface. God had to shift the currents slightly, for this would cause the volcanoes to wane and begin to die. Eruptions at this stage only produce scalding water and steam, which would gradually transform the atmosphere into one that Man could breathe.

Eventually all this took place, and proof that it was engineered is the fact that the water content of the volcanic eruptions came from magma and the natural water table of Earth's crust. We stated earlier that God used asteroids and comets to inject Earth with water, and now we can see why!

The part played by water validates Genesis 2.5-6, which says God, before establishing plants and seeds, engineered "a mist from the earth, and [it] watered the whole face of the ground." If we substitute steam for "mist," then the Genesis account exactly fits the science.

The steam would eventually have condensed and produced rainfall that watered the whole ground. This would have created a "firmament" (Genesis 1.6), a term that literally means an expanse of water beneath vapours. If we substitute atmosphere for vapours, then Genesis does indeed explain how our atmosphere and the water that covers most of our planet were created.

The waning of volcanoes dispelled the darkness produced by volcanic ash and replaced it with light. This was also part of God's plan, for Genesis 1.4 says, "God said, Let there be light…and God divided the light from the darkness."

Biblical scholars believe this means God created night and day, but they overlook the fact that, prior to God creating light, Earth must have been in total darkness. We have shown that the darkness was produced by volcanic ash that God had to dispel in order to create light.

This operation took place on the first day and was immediately followed by the creation of a firmament. This, as we pointed out earlier, created the right atmosphere for Man.

* * * * * * *

Dissolved in the water that had been brought from deep within Earth to the surface were a great variety of chemical substances. Some came from the same deep source as magma, others were dissolved from the rocks through which the hot water passed on its way to the surface. Amongst these were compounds of nitrogen and sulphur, often in such concentrations that the water could serve as food for very simple organisms.

Scientists believe the chemical compounds for organisms existed on Earth some three billion years ago. This was largely because the Moon had helped to form cells.

The collision between Earth and Thea forced vast quantities of gas and minerals from Earth's interior to the surface. Iron reacted with gases such as oxygen and methane and this, together with lightning, created the conditions in which cells could form. The Moon's spin, together with its gravitational force, caused Earth to slow down and cool. This allowed oceans to form, and the Moon's gravitational force created tides.

The ebb and flow of tides acted as a catalyst for life, according to Professor John Sutherland. When the tide went out, the Sun dried the pools. The power of the Sun (ultra-violet light) changed the structure of chemicals within cells and created RNA (messenger DNA).

This proves that the collision between Earth and Thea was crucial for the success of God's plan, and did not happen by chance. It is also another example showing that God calculated the Sun's output to perfection.

CHAPTER FIVE

THE CURRENT STATE OF THE UNIVERSE

Part 1

THE SUN IS ONLY one of the 100 billion stars that are visible in our galaxy, and this number is dwarfed after its rate of rotation is taken into account, for this suggests it has a mass equivalent to 400 billion stars. Despite this huge number of stars, our galaxy has gravitational stability. This is not a quality possessed by all spiral galaxies. M64, for example, is called the Evil Eye because a billion years ago a galaxy crashed into it, distorting its structure. Its stars orbit in the same direction, which is usual in a galaxy, but the gas in its outer regions moves in the opposite direction. This leads to constant collisions, giving the galaxy its "black-eyed" appearance.

The Sun is situated two-thirds distant (30,000 light years) from the centre of our galaxy, but unlike stars in analogous regions in M64 it is not troubled by collisions. Every object in our galaxy rotates in the same direction.

The Sun orbits the centre of our galaxy at a speed of 155 miles per second, but our galaxy is so vast that the Sun takes 250 million years to complete one circuit. During its circuit the Sun is in no danger of colliding with other stars or star systems because it is so far from the centre.

This means God designed our galaxy in such a manner as to ensure that the Solar System (and therefore Earth) has a trouble-free existence, and as our galaxy is 13.2 billion years old, He must have begun to design it shortly after the formation of the universe.

But God's design had to encompass the entire universe, because our galaxy is only one of 100 billion galaxies, and many of these are much larger than our own. To ensure that our galaxy has a trouble-free existence, God had to arrange galaxies in particular formations, and observations show that galaxies – and the stars within galaxies – are clustering together in three recognisable forms that constitute an ascending or hierarchical order of grouping.

The clustering of stars in our galaxy may be regarded as typical. The lowest order of clustering comprises associations of stars that have just emerged from stellar nurseries, consequently they are the youngest stars. Less than 100 associations are known, and all are in the spiral arms of our galaxy because these, being rich in dust and gas, are the spawning grounds for new stars.

The lowest order comprises associations of stars that have just emerged from stellar nurseries, consequently they are the youngest stars. Less than 100 associations are known, and all are in the spiral arms of our galaxy because these, being rich in dust and gas, are the spawning grounds for new stars.

Open clusters are the next highest order of clustering. Whereas an association of stars contains probably less than 100 members, open clusters can contain as many as 1,000. Stars in open clusters are older than those in associations but are young on the astronomical time-scale – clusters such as the Pleiades are probably less than 50 million years old. Consequently open clusters are found in the far regions of the galaxy, but are closer to us than associations.

More than 1,000 open clusters are known, but in all probability there are thousands of such clusters scattered about our galaxy.

Globular clusters are the highest order of clustering. These clusters differ in almost every respect from open clusters and associations. Some 120 are known, and probably represent the great majority of globular clusters in our galaxy.

Globular clusters are immense (175-350 light years in diameter) and contain tens of thousands to 100,000 or more stars. They are the oldest stellar formations in our galaxy because they are comprised of a type of star that our galaxy can no longer create.

Since globular clusters contain the oldest stars, they are found at the centre of the galaxy. Each star orbits the gravitational centre of the cluster, while the entire cluster orbits about the centre of the galaxy, probably taking about 100 million years to make one circuit of the galaxy.

Galaxies have likewise clustered together, and their clustering – like that of the stars – can be arranged in an ascending or hierarchical order.

Our galaxy is the major member of a close triplet comprising the Large and Small Magellanic Clouds, but the triplet is only a minor feature in a larger grouping, the Local Group of galaxies, which includes at least twenty recognised members. The overall diameter of the Local Group is at least 5 million light years, its thickness almost 2 million light years. More than a dozen other groups have been identified within a radius of 30 million light years from the Group.

Even this grouping is small compared with other clusters. These contain hundreds or thousands of members. The nearest to us is in the constellation of Virgo, at a distance of about 40 million light years. This cluster includes two main components, one highly concentrated. Even larger and richer clusters have been observed at greater distances. The nearest of these is in the constellation of Coma, at an estimated distance of 200 million light years. It has a diameter in excess of 15 million light years, but half its total population of several thousand (possibly tens of thousands) galaxies is concentrated within a diameter of 5 million light years.

But these clusters are dwarfed by superclusters! Several thousands of the brighter galaxies form a roughly ellipsoidal supersystem, the centre of which is marked by the Virgo cluster. The overall diameter of this supercluster is about 100 million light years and its maximum thickness 30-40 million light years. The Local Group, including our galaxy, is only a minor condensation not far from the southern edge.

This "Local Supercluster" is small, however, compared with the CFA2 Great Wall, which is 750 million light years long, 250 million light years wide and 20 million light years thick. However, this is barely half the size of the Sloan Great Wall, which is 1,412.5 million light years in length, and is the largest known structure in the universe.

The identical hierarchical orders of clustering for stars and galaxies can only mean they are being guided into position by an unseen force. The force must be gravity, but current theories regarding gravity do not explain how stars and galaxies can manœuvre themselves into formations, therefore we have to re-examine the nature of gravity.

It used to be thought that gravitational force derived from the mass of an object, but this did not explain why objects too far apart to be affected by their different masses obeyed the laws of gravity.

Einstein believed he had found the answer with the idea that our resistance to a sudden acceleration (inertial mass) is no different to the sensation we would feel if gravity was suddenly increased – our feet would be 'tied' to the ground. This meant gravity had mass.

Einstein then applied this example to cosmology. If Earth was dragged upwards at great speed, only people at the North Pole would experience acceleration as gravity, so to remedy this Einstein proposed that Earth exists in a fourth dimension, which he termed spacetime.

Einstein then extended the scope of spacetime to cover the universe. It became a four-dimensional rubber sheet on which sat every celestial object. Matter, however, warps spacetime, in the same way that a heavy object dents a sheet, therefore light, which always takes the shortest route from A to B, would have to bend whenever it came to a warp. Such a bending was observed during the total eclipse of May 1919, and thereafter the old concepts of gravity were replaced by Einstein's theory that gravity is spacetime warps.

The effect of these warps is to bring together regions of the universe separated by many light years, and this accounted for gravity influencing the movements of objects too remote to be attracted to each other by sheer mass. Einstein's theory thus solved the problem that had baffled earlier scientists.

However, it never occurred to Einstein (or any other scientist) that gravity was aware that it was creating planets, stars and galaxies that conform to the laws of physics, and in this respect Einstein (and every other scientist) failed to realise the full significance of his mathematical proof, viz., if gravity can be expressed in mathematical terms, and mathematical constants denote the 'mind' of Nature, then gravity cannot be mindless.

Given that gravity is mindful, then it must be purposeful. This means the effects it produces are deliberate.

For gravity to have a mind it must have programmes. These have to be written, consequently the intelligence of gravity derives from the author of the programmes.

Who could have written the programmes? There is only one answer: God.

* * * * * * *

Where could God have installed the programmes? They have to be inside every atom, and since the sub-atomic world is a void except for a central nucleus and orbiting electrons, God must have installed the programmes in one or other of these objects.

The nucleus contains an equal number of neutrons and protons.

Neutrons are negatively charged and protons are positively charged. Ordinarily neutrons would fly away from each other, and likewise protons, because a law of physics states "like poles repel", but they are held together by the 'strong nuclear force.'

The 'strong nuclear force' is neither electrical nor gravitational, yet its tremendous binding power combines the properties of both. When two nuclei are brought close together, their positive charges repel each other, but when they come so close together that they almost touch, the 'strong nuclear force' overcomes the positive electromagnetism that keeps the nuclei apart, and fuses them together.

With neutrons and protons tightly bound together, the nucleus contains the equivalent of a computer's hard disk. Such disks have to be magnetised, otherwise they would be unable to retain any information. We believe the 'strong nuclear force' performs the same function as magnetism, giving the nucleus a hard disk on which God could have written programmes.

These programmes convert the nucleus into a micro-computer!

* * * * * * *

We have accounted for the source of gravity that affects the universe, but it does not explain the order and harmony that exists within the atom. Electrons are minute compared with the size of the nucleus, but the nucleus is only one billionth the size of the atom, hence the distance between the nucleus and orbiting electrons is so great that they are not influenced by their different masses. Add to this the fact that the interior of the atom is a vacuum, and it is clear that neither Einstein's nor any other scientific definition of gravity accounts for gravitational stability within the atom.

Furthermore, the nucleus is positively charged but electrons are negatively charged and try to enter the nucleus (a law of physics states "unlike poles attract"). If electrons succeeded in gaining entry, they would convert protons to neutrons, thus neutralising the positive charge, and all the information on the hard disk would be lost. Therefore God had to provide the nucleus with a defence, and indeed it emits an electrostatic force that repels electrons.

This force is equivalent to a series of commands telling electrons not to come too close – to remain in their orbits.

The orbiting electrons are kept apart by their negative charge (another law of physics states "like poles repel"), which avoids collisions. They also rotate on their axes, creating a gravitational pull that balances the gravitational pull of the nucleus.

Thus gravity maintains stability within the atom, but its source is the nucleus, which issues commands that cross the vacuum.

These commands, together with the laws of physics, must derive from programmes that God installed in the nucleus. This explains why every problem was foreseen and overcome.

Chapter Six
The Origin of Matter

Part 1

When did God write the programmes? This requires us to consider the origin of all the matter in the universe.

The universe was created by an enormous explosion – the Big Bang – but scientists have been unable to agree on the cause of the Big Bang or what existed beforehand. This means they cannot account for the origin of matter.

Einstein thought he had done so because one strand of his Theory of Relativity says mass and energy are only different forms of the same phenomenon ($E=mc^2$). In other words, mass can be produced from a void. According to Einstein, if a strong beam of energy shot past a heavy atomic nucleus, then the beam of energy would disappear into the strong electrical field of energy generated by the atomic nucleus. In its place an electron and a positron would appear, hence energy in the form of a beam would have changed into the mass of two electrons. However, Einstein could not explain how the energy beam and the nucleus were created and so he could not account for the matter that was discharged into space by the Big Bang.

Therefore we have to assume that space, prior to the Big Bang, was not a void. But if matter was present, how did it come into existence?

Scientists believe it could have arisen either spontaneously – a physical manifestation of pure energy – or from a chaotic situation. For example, water molecules exist in three different states – solid (ice), liquid and gas (vapour) – and only require a change of temperature to change from one state to another, therefore water molecules existed before the change of temperature. By analogy it only required a change of temperature – heat from the Big Bang – to change the fundamental particles – quarks – into protons and neutrons – the particles within the nucleus – therefore quarks existed before the Big Bang.

However, this does not explain how quarks came into existence, nor the fact that atoms behave in an orderly and predictable manner – the antithesis of mindless energy and chaos!

The behaviour of atoms gives rise to the laws of physics. These enable scientists to predict the movements of planets, stars, galaxies, etc., proving there is order and harmony in the universe.

If a mindless or chaotic situation had existed before the Big Bang, none of this order and harmony would have been possible, because the Big Bang would only have produced another mindless or chaotic situation. Mindlessness and chaos can only lead to mindlessness and chaos until an external force acts upon them to produce order.

Therefore the order and harmony in the universe is the result of this force programming atoms to behave in an orderly manner, and it must have done so prior to the Big Bang.

We have proved that God programmed atoms, and now we know when He did so.

Part 2

Clearly God programmed atoms for a purpose, and the fact that the sub-atomic world remained intact after the Big Bang meant the programmes continued to operate. Given that commands from the nucleus – gravity – can cross a vacuum, it follows that nuclei were able to give directions across the voids in the universe, consequently we can deduce the instructions in many of the programmes by reference to events in the immediate aftermath of the Big Bang, and the manner in which the universe has unfolded down to the present day.

According to the standard model of the universe that scientists have drawn up, the universe inflated slightly before giving way to the force of the Big Bang. The inflation is necessary to account for the fact that everywhere the temperature of the universe is a few degrees above absolute zero. If the universe had expanded as a result of the Big Bang, then the temperature would vary - some regions would be hotter than others - but if the universe inflated before the Big Bang, then the temperature would be constant.

However, scientists cannot explain why the universe should have inflated, but if we assume that one of the programmes in the nucleus showed the position of every atom within an object, then it would act as a command to atoms to maintain their stations, and only give way when the force of the Big Bang became irresistible.

To maintain their stations, nuclei have to co-ordinate by communicating with each other, consequently they had to create channels of communication that span the universe. This would account for gravity affecting the movement of celestial bodies too far apart to be influenced by their respective masses.

We have thus superseded Einstein's theory of spacetime with one that not only solves the problem he addressed, but also gives meaning and purpose to gravity.

* * * * * * *

The communications between nuclei lead to the formation of stars, planets, galaxies, etc., consequently the channels of communication contain an immense amount of data. Since this data affects every part of the universe, we can liken the channels to an internet broadband facility on a universal scale.

Internet users have screen names and addresses that are registered with their internet service provider (ISP). The same arrangement must apply to nuclei, therefore we have to regard God as internet service provider to the universe!

Part 3

The programmes are directing atoms throughout the universe to return to their original positions, and this not only explains the clusterings of stars and galaxies that we examined earlier, but also solves a conundrum in the scientists' standard model that has recently come to light. Instrument readings have shown that the space between galaxies is not a void, as required by the model, but contains energy that causes stars and galaxies to move in ways contrary to those set out in the model. Scientists cannot account for the existence of this energy, and have termed it 'dark flow,' but the channels of communication between nuclei would emit energy, and the commands they carry would instigate movements of celestial bodies that vary from the predictions in the model of the universe. Therefore 'dark flow' is a natural consequence of atoms being hurled into space and endeavouring to restore the situation that existed before the Big Bang.

The process of restoration consists of concentrating all the material in the universe in one small area. This process can be seen operating on two different scales. On the grand scale stars and galaxies are clustering together, as we showed earlier, and on the small scale, black holes at the centres of galaxies are hoovering up vast amounts of stellar material.

This is the first time anyone has found an intelligent use for black holes, but they are a product of gravity, and therefore must have an intelligent purpose.

Scientists consider black holes to be a theoretical concept because they cannot be seen – their gravitational pull is so great that light cannot escape – consequently they are unclear as to the nature and properties of black holes. They believe that at the centre of a black hole density is infinite because matter has been crushed to zero volume, creating a point of infinite gravitational force called a 'singularity'.

Our theory says an object comprising all the atoms in the universe must have existed before the Big Bang, therefore this explosion would have created an equally great implosion, in accordance with a fundamental law of physics that states every action produces an equally great opposite reaction. Therefore fifty per cent of the object's matter imploded whilst the other half exploded.

The force of the implosion/explosion would have been far greater than that of a supernova because it released the pent-up power of every atom. Therefore the implosion would have had sufficient force to compress half the object's matter, and since supernovæ of much less force have created black holes, the implosion would have created the largest imaginable black hole.

The creation of the black hole would have been completed in an instant, hence matter hurled into space by the explosion would have immediately felt its gravitational pull. The pull would have been sufficient to begin the process whereby vaporised matter condensed into gas clouds and then formed stars and galaxies.

This chain of events overcomes another drawback to the scientists' model of the universe: its failure to account for the vast number of stars and galaxies in the universe. Calculations have shown that there is insufficient matter in the universe to exert the necessary gravitational pull. To overcome this objection, the model allows for the creation of black holes immediately after the Big Bang, but they are small and their influence is local, therefore scientists have invented an invisible substance: 'cold, dark matter' (CDM). According to the scientists, CDM comprises ninety per cent of the matter in the universe, and would have the necessary gravitational effect, but they are unable to account for its existence, give any details of its composition, or explain why it is cold and dark.

Part 4

Our theory that the Big Bang obliterated an object accounts for the creation of stars and galaxies within the necessary time-frame, but leads to the formation of a super-massive black hole in which, according to scientists, matter is crushed to zero volume.

However, this assumes that gravity is a mindless and inexorable force, whereas we have proved it is a form of intelligence because it contains commands between nuclei. Moreover, atoms would only gradually have given way under the force of the implosion (an equal and opposite reaction to that of atoms caught by the explosion). Finally, atoms have built-in protection against being crushed. The orbiting electrons are negatively charged, which means their polarities are identical and keep atoms apart. Likewise nuclei – the 'minds' of atoms – cannot be crushed because they are positively charged and repel each other. These defences are so logical and sophisticated that they must have been devised by God to preserve the integrity of atoms.

Nevertheless, gravity is a weak force compared with other forces of energy, and the energy of the implosion would have overcome the repulsion between electrons, causing atoms to crush each other. This, according to science, forces electrons into the nucleus and leads to the neutralisation of protons, but our theory says that, as this would lead to the loss of all the information stored in the nucleus, God must have provided it with a defence against this possibility.

The defence resides in the properties of the 'strong nuclear force'. Its binding power pervades the hard disk, acting as a shield, and because it is neither electrical nor gravitational, electrons cannot penetrate it.

Furthermore, the interior of the nucleus is incredibly dense, equivalent to 100,000 tons per cubic millimetre. Add to this the first law of energy, which states 'energy can neither be created nor destroyed,' and mass is another form of energy, it follows that the nucleus cannot be crushed out of existence.

Since not even the unimaginably strong compression that takes place within a black hole can damage the interior of the nucleus, its programmes can operate under any conditions.

However, the energy generated by the implosion would have been so great that it would have forced nuclei to fuse. This would seem to render nuclei completely inoperative, undoing all God's work.

Such is not the case, however! Black holes have gravitational force, proving that fused nuclei retain channels of communication with outside bodies. Moreover, the gravitational strength of a black hole is far greater than that which it exerted when it was a star – even light cannot escape – and this means the implosion strengthened the command structure amongst nuclei (such a structure has to exist, because commands between nuclei necessitate a chain of command – a hierarchy – and its new-found strength must derive from the fusion of nuclei, because this would create a new hierarchy containing higher ranking officers with greater powers).

Consequently within a black hole there are opposing forces. On the one hand there is the combination of energy generated by the implosion plus gravity, and these, taken to their logical conclusion, will crush matter into a 'singularity'. Opposed to these forces is gravity that keeps open the channels of communication between nuclei. This form of gravity is therefore anti-gravity!

Within anti-gravity the laws set out in Einstein's Theory of Relativity are reversed. Thus objects normally travel below the speed of light because Einstein's theory stated that anything containing mass cannot travel faster than the speed of light, but in anti-gravity they have no constraints. They can travel at an infinitely great speed and traverse the universe in an instant.

Therefore within a region of anti-gravity, time and distance have no meaning. If an object fell into a black hole and entered one of these channels of communication, it could instantly find itself on the other side of the universe. This is equivalent to time-travel, because the object could emerge billions of light years ahead or behind the time it entered the black hole.

We have thus discovered a logical basis for a theory first set out by Einstein that black holes could be a means of accomplishing time-travel. However, Einstein could only predicate this idea by suggesting that black holes warped space and time to such an extent that they folded back on themselves, and brought together two regions of the universe that otherwise would be separated by many light years, but we pointed out earlier that Einstein's ideas were superficial because it never occurred to him that gravity had a meaningful purpose. Our theory, by contrast, embodies a purpose for time-travel, because it permits instantaneous communication across light years, and enables nuclei to co-ordinate their actions throughout the universe as a prelude to restoring the object that was destroyed in the Big Bang.

The differences between our theory and those of Einstein (and every other scientist) arise from the fact that he assumed the keys that unlocked the secrets of the universe lay within the universe, whereas we placed the universe in a much wider context and found that the keys lay outside.

The key to understanding gravity is to regard it as a combination of forces. It is primarily a force of attraction, the purpose of which is to align atoms as per the genome in each nucleus, but this force is subject to the commands between nuclei, and their channels of communication are kept open by anti-gravity, the properties of which allow commands to be transmitted instantly to anywhere in the universe. The channels are infinitesimally thin strands within gravity, equivalent to (but far thinner than) a fibre-optic strand within a cable.

Part 5

Nuclei within black holes not only preserve their integrity but also gain added authority and strength. They use their new-found strength to attract material from neighbouring stars, and this hoovering up process concentrates an enormous amount of matter in a small space. Since God must first clear up the damage created by the Big Bang, the actions of black holes fit in perfectly. They are the first stage of a tidying up operation that will ultimately concentrate all the matter in the universe in one small area.

It should come as no surprise that black holes fit in with God's wishes, because they were created by gravity, which contains commands that He wrote.

Consequently the creation of a super-massive black hole immediately after the Big Bang suited God perfectly, but this is where our theory has to overcome another major drawback: scientists have not detected a black hole at the centre of the universe.

In their view this means the black hole never existed, because its density, like that of every black hole, would have been so great as to render it unchangeable and eternal. Without the black hole, an object could not have been destroyed by the Big Bang, and this destroys our theory regarding the creation of matter.

However, we believe scientists have not detected the black hole because it no longer exists! The channels of communication to which we referred earlier constituted weaknesses in its structure, and the black hole could not withstand these weaknesses.

The gravitational pull of the black hole was so great that it attracted most – perhaps as much as ninety per cent – of the matter hurled into space. As matter fell into the black hole, its temperature rose by millions of degrees Centigrade. Heat equates to energy, therefore the black hole had to contain an enormous increase in energy, and could not afford a weakness. Consequently a time came when it was unstable, but its gravitational strength forced it to absorb more matter. Gravity created the black hole and gravity destroyed it.

After its destruction the black hole would have fragmented into localised black holes, and this is where our theory links up with the scientists' model.

Therefore the background radiation that scientists believe is an echo of the Big Bang is actually an echo of the destruction of the black hole.

Scientists have traced the radiation to its source, and on this basis they are certain that it originated 13.7 billion years ago. But as this is only the date when the black hole exploded, the Big Bang must have occurred billions of years earlier. Consequently the universe is far older than anyone has imagined.

Part 6

The hierarchical order amongst nuclei generates commands that produce the hierarchical clustering amongst stars and galaxies. Commands between nuclei derive from programmes God wrote, consequently the clustering is all part of His plan.

Once we can fit the main features of the universe into God's plan, then others must do likewise. Since the late 1980s, astronomers have noticed that many galaxies are being drawn towards the Norma cluster, 222 million light years away. The reason for this is unknown, hence the source has been dubbed 'The Great Attractor'. However, this flow calls to mind 'dark flow', the term given to the movement of millions of galaxies spanning billions of light years that does not conform to the standard model of the universe, but which we showed results from commands issued by nuclei to align atoms in their formations prior to the Big Bang.

At the outermost fringes of the universe, galaxies are receding at faster velocities than those closer to home, and this has given rise to the Hubble Constant – the greater the distance of a galaxy, the greater its recession velocity. This in turn has given rise to the theory that the universe will expand forever.

According to this theory, the more remote galaxies become, the greater the gravitational force needed to halt their recession, and in due course the force required will exceed the gravitational force exerted by matter in these regions. When this occurs, nothing can stop the recession of these galaxies.

Another theory supports this outcome. It predicates the existence of 'dark energy'. This type of energy is the antithesis of gravity because it forces objects away from each other. It was conceived as a means of explaining why the oldest galaxies are receding at ever-increasing velocities when they should have lost the momentum they acquired after the Big Bang. If 'dark energy' actually exists, and is stronger than gravity in the outermost regions of the universe, then it would force the universe to expand forever.

However, such an outcome would be the very opposite to that which God wishes to achieve, and indeed no instruments have detected 'dark energy'. Furthermore, both theories are based on a misunderstanding of the nature of gravity, and underestimate its strength. Finally, black holes and quasars at the centres of these galaxies will in due course use up all their fuel – neighbouring stars – and lose power, causing the galaxies to lose momentum and fall back to the centre of gravity of the universe. In the process they will merge or collide with other galaxies, and thus fall in with God's plan by contributing to the clustering that we described earlier.

Chapter Seven
The Big Bang

Part 1

The only explanation for the immediate aftermath of the Big Bang and the current state of the universe is that the Big Bang destroyed an object God had designed, but the fact that every atom – every star and galaxy – is endeavouring to return to the state that existed prior to the Big Bang is even more significant.

It means they are trying to reverse the consequences of the Big Bang, and this has awesome implications.

The Big Bang could not have been part of God's plan – it was not meant to happen!

After the Big Bang God quickly set about creating the perfect environment for Man and then creating Man, consequently there has to be a connection between the cause of the Big Bang and God's creation of Man.

Clearly we must be essential to Him, and this relationship predates the Big Bang.

We may therefore assume that God designed the object but required an agency – Man – to carry out the physical tasks that construction entailed, and there are passages in Genesis that support this idea.

God had to invest Man with God-like powers so that he could carry out his allotted tasks, and in Genesis 1.26 God said He created Man "in our image, after our likeness."

God-like qualities call for God-like life-spans, and Genesis duly records incredible life-spans for Adam, Noah, Methuselah and many others.

God only required a certain number of people to work on His project, therefore He had to restrict Man's population and govern his evolution, otherwise he would attain such numbers and acquire such powers as could overwhelm God. This equates to God's command forbidding Adam and Eve to eat the fruit of the Tree of Life.

Once the project had been completed, God would have divested Man of his God-like powers and erased from his memory information that He did not wish Man to possess. This equates to God's command forbidding Adam and Eve to eat the fruit of the Tree of Knowledge.

Man would therefore have been as innocent as Adam and Eve. He would also have been living in an area that God had specially created for him, an area that corresponds to the Garden of Eden.

These references show that Genesis, although considered to be an account of the origin of Man on Earth, is actually two histories in one.

* * * * * * *

The area in which our forerunners dwelt would have provided God with the information He needed to design Earth. It would also have helped Him shape the environment in which we would dwell.

We may assume God preserved samples of the organisms and creatures that had inhabited the world in which our forerunners had dwelt, and could transfer them to Earth at key stages of evolution.

These transfers must be the creative acts listed in Genesis, and Genesis offers implicit support for this idea. Biblical scholars, after studying its text, believe the sudden appearance of plants, following God's intervention after Earth had suffered a catastrophe that left it in a "primitive state", meant the life-germ of seeds did not perish in the catastrophe, hence with the restoration of dry land and light, Earth would "bring forth" as described. Our amendment is that God preserved samples of seeds from the region in which Man's forerunners had dwelt and, once He had completed structural changes to Earth at its formative ("primitive") stage, transplanted them to Earth.

Clearly God had to replicate on Earth the environment in which our forerunners had dwelt, but whereas He had created their world by design and engineering, Earth was created by a natural force – gravity – which endowed it with very different geological, geographical and climatic conditions.

Every organism and creature had to adapt to these conditions. This meant God could 'sow' the seeds of life, but evolution would proceed along its natural course and at its natural pace. However, God had already determined the goal for evolution – to create an environment that was suitable for Man – and had a finishing date in mind, therefore He had to be able to control evolution, and this explains why He inserted a soul ("nephesh") into every living thing.

Part 2

The fact that God had to recreate Man means that our forerunners must have been obliterated in the Big Bang. Since Man would not have opted for self-annihilation, we have to assume that he was not responsible for the explosion, therefore someone else must have existed alongside God and Man, and it was he that caused the catastrophe.

Where there is God (good) there is the Devil (evil), and he is the additional factor that enables us to outline a sequence of events that leads practically by force to the Big Bang.

God required Man to construct the object He had designed, but the Devil was determined to destroy anything God had created. However, the Devil – like God – can only carry out his plans through Man, therefore he had to tempt the very people who had built the object to bring about its destruction, and this he eventually succeeded in doing.

The cause of the Big Bang can therefore be summed up in one word: sabotage.

* * * * * * *

There is an oblique reference to our scenario in the Bible, for both Ezekiel 28.12-15 and Isaiah 14.9-14 refer to a testing and fall of angels prior to the creation of Heaven and Earth. Angels are traditionally regarded as guardians of Man, providing him with comfort, support, guidance, and protection. Traditions are usually based on facts, therefore we may assume that God, after creating Man, assigned to him angels as guardians. This rôle placed angels in supervisory positions as construction got under way, and if the Devil was amongst them – he first appears in the Bible as "an angel of light" (2 Corinthians 11.14) – then he would be in an ideal position to engineer the catastrophe.

Our scenario contradicts the biblical view of God as all-seeing and all-knowing, but this is an unavoidable consequence of its inherent logic. It portrays the Devil as an entity or force that has a right to exist. Furthermore, that God and the Devil are almost equal, for God possesses superior strength and must prevail in the long run, but occasionally the Devil may thwart Him. Quite possibly they should be regarded as opposite sides of the same coin. This would mean God can punish the Devil but cannot destroy him, and would provide a logical basis for the statement in Revelation 20.3 that God could only sentence the Devil to a term of imprisonment, and then had to set him free.

* * * * * * *

There are references to our scenario in Genesis. The world on which our forerunners dwelt was comprised of atoms God had programmed. The programmes give life to every atom, and in that sense our forerunners dwelt on a living world. The distinguishing feature of such a world is that it evolves, consequently our forerunners had to be capable of adapting to changing conditions. They also had to develop their talents and skills to the utmost, as we do. Therefore they required free will, but once God had endowed them with free will, He could not reveal Himself to them or constrain them in any way. However, free will spans both good and evil, so it was only a matter of time before evil (the Devil) entered our forerunners' thoughts. This accords with the story of Adam and Eve.

The Devil had been in a position to acquire intimate knowledge concerning God's project, and this was knowledge God did not want Man to acquire. His displeasure at discovering our forerunners had heeded the Devil would have been obvious – as plain as His displeasure with Adam and Eve – and the punishment – banishment from the Garden of Eden – would have been the same.

God's Schedule

CHAPTER ONE

ADAM AND EVE IN THE GARDEN OF EDEN

Part 1

GOD RECREATED MAN SO that he could reconstruct the object destroyed by the Big Bang. It must have been to avoid any mention of this catastrophe that God omitted to explain in the Bible why He created Man, but He must have been mindful of the part that our forerunners had played in bringing it about, because it explains the strictures he placed upon Man (personified by Adam and Eve).

In Genesis 2.17 God told Man, "But of the tree of the knowledge of good and evil thou shalt not eat," which means God will withhold certain knowledge from Man until he has risen above temptation.

To reach this level, Man has to adhere to God's expressed will, therefore he has not only to be aware of God but also possess a spiritual sense, and we showed in Part 3 of our opening chapter that one of the operations God performed produced such a sense.

After this and other operations, God declared in Genesis 1.26 that He had made Man "in our image, after our likeness." We stated in the previous chapter that this verse refers to our God-like forerunners, but we also pointed out that Genesis is two histories in one, and this is another example of how it interwove the histories, because the Bible says we also have "likeness." It is our tri-unity and moral nature. Man is "spirit and soul and body" (I Thessalonians 5.23). "Spirit" is the part of Man that "knows" (I Corinthians 2.11) and, allied to spiritual creation, gives him God-consciousness. "Soul" is the seat of his emotions, desires and affections (Psalms 42.1-6). The body is the seat of the senses – the means by which the spirit and soul have world-consciousness.

These qualities enable Man to be aware of God. He is, in fact, the only creature with God-consciousness, and this creates a gulf between Man and the primates that Huxley described as "a divergence practically infinite."

We could not, therefore, have acquired such awareness by evolving naturally from the primates, and this is irrefutable proof that God created us.

* * * * * * *

God confirmed that Man was pure – without sin – by exempting him from the need to make atonement. This is a ritual in which God demands a blood sacrifice as implying confession of sin and its just desert (death), but in respect of Man God said, "Behold, I have given you every herb bearing seed which is upon the face of Earth, and every tree, in the which is the fruit of a tree yielding seed; to you these shall be for meat. And to every beast of the earth, and to every fowl of the air, and to everything that creepeth upon the earth wherein there is life [blood], I have given every green herb for meat" (Genesis 1.29-30).

These words might seem to indicate that God intended Man to be a vegetarian, but He would have known that Man was descended from mammalian omnivores. Furthermore, He would have realised that Man needed more protein than fruit and plants could provide on account of his greater brain power and ability to perform more complex tasks. Therefore His command can only have one meaning: Man does not have to atone for anything (does not have to shed blood).

* * * * * * *

Adam and Eve personified the purity and innocence of early Man. However, we know from the account given in Genesis that this state of affairs did not last long. Contrary to God's command, they began to think for themselves, succumbed to the Devil's temptation, and ate "the apple from the Tree of Knowledge". When God discovered what they had done, He banished them from the Garden.

This leads to the following conclusions: God can command Man, but cannot make him obey; God will reveal the knowledge that Man needs, but cannot blind him to other ideas; finally, God cannot prevent the Devil from tempting Man.

These are contradictory conclusions, yet they express God's intention. To explain this conundrum, we have to realise that Man can only disobey God's commands, and can only succumb to temptation, if he has the will to do so – free will – hence God must have granted Man free will. But why give Man free will if it gives him the opportunity to go wrong?

This gives rise to a related question: why – given that Man was receptive to temptation – did God place him in an environment that was accessible to the Devil?

The answer to both these questions is that God deliberately exposed Man to temptation! He did so because Man's forerunners had succumbed to the Devil and destroyed the object He had designed, so He has to ensure that we have sufficient strength of character not to succumb again. The only way to achieve this is to leave us open to temptation.

This explains why life is a constant test of character. Every aspect of life confronts us with a choice between good and evil. Every decision we make is either good or bad, and our character will determine the choice.

Free will is double-edged. Its negative side has been described as the right to do wrong, but its positive side gives rise to daring, enterprise, imagination, and the belief that one's possibilities are limitless.

Therefore God imbued us with free will to raise our thoughts far above those of other creatures, and to strengthen our character by exposing us to temptation.

When God endowed Man with free will, He effectively released the Devil. This means God needs the Devil to strengthen Man's character by exposing him to every type of temptation, and the Devil needs God so that Man can compare evil with good. This echoes the point we made in the previous chapter that God and the Devil should be regarded as opposite sides of the same coin. One cannot exist without the other, and both have a right to exist.

Now we know why God allowed the Devil access to Adam and Eve!

* * * * * * *

Free will allows us to consider possibilities imaginatively. Imagination is the highest level of intelligence. It is a leap of logic that allows us to see and explore possibilities far beyond the realm of exact calculation, hence intelligence can be defined as ideas born of free will.

Ideas have to be converted into files and stored in our memory before they can serve the intellect, therefore they have to be converted into thoughts that register on our mind and create files. Personality generates thoughts, therefore free will must be a programme embedded in personality.

Free will should be regarded as a search engine analogous to those found in computers. Creatures use their search engines to explore the range of options that will enable them to survive. We have advanced far beyond this level, and use our search engines to explore the range of ideas on intellectual subjects.

Therefore we have a booster attached to our search engines that we could never have acquired through natural evolution.

* * * * * * *

God must have installed free will in Adam (*Homo erectus*) and Eve (*Homo sapiens*) because it raised their levels of thinking far above that of earliest Man, but since its range of thought covered good and evil, God had to install mechanisms in the mind that enable Him to monitor its exercise.

This means God has to have a complete record of our lives so that He can see how we coped with the tests of character to which life subjects us. Proof that we possess a complete record is furnished by people who, under hypnosis, have been able to recall facts and other details they had completely forgotten.

Clearly certain processes in the mind ensure that we do not forget anything we have committed to memory. For example, a traumatic shock to the mind can give rise to amnesia or memory-loss, but it is only a temporary condition because the mind is able to repair the damage. No one, however, has been able to explain how such a shock causes memory-loss or how the mind repairs the damage. We believe the shock disrupted the directory on which every file is registered. Once the directory is damaged, it is impossible to locate files and extract information from them until the damage is repaired.

The task of repairing the damage begins almost immediately, but it takes time to complete. In the meantime we absorb new knowledge and accumulate fresh memories. This can only be explained by the presence of a back-up system.

The system must be situated in a region of the mind that was undamaged and contains a new directory on which files can be registered. Thoughts are automatically switched to the 'window' in which the directory is situated, allowing new files to be registered and fresh memories created.

* * * * * * *

However desirable total recall may appear to be, it runs counter to the development of ideas and personality.

Personality evolves. When we are adults we need to forget childish behaviour. We also have to forget ideas that have become superseded. Therefore we have to be able to erase from our consciousness childish standards of behaviour and outmoded ideas.

The trigger for erasure is a thought telling our mind that a particular idea or form of behaviour is outdated. The thought contains keys that identify the file(s) to be deleted. Once they are deleted, we cannot access them anymore.

The files have not, however, been deleted from our mind. By analogy with computers, they have been despatched to the recycle bin. They will not appear in the 'windows' of our mind, but we can reinstate them, if we so desire. However, computer operators can empty the recycle bin, which deletes files from the directory, but we do not have this option.

This is because God needs to know how we coped with life, therefore He needs to have a complete record of our lives. Free will enables us to explore all the possibilities life has to offer, and these test our character. Each of us responds differently to the tests because we have free will, and therefore God needs to know how each of us responded.

It follows that God has to be able to access our files (memories) after we pass on, and indeed He said in the Bible that He is able to pass judgement on everyone. No one, however, has been able to imagine how He can do this, but we shall show that it presents no problems.

CHAPTER TWO
THE HUMAN SOUL

Part 1

WE CANNOT POSSIBLY LEARN in one lifetime all the knowledge that enables us to play our part in God's plan, nor can we acquire in one lifetime the level of spirituality that places us above temptation. Therefore we have to live through many – perhaps thousands – of lifetimes, and this means the human soul has to be immortal.

The soul also has to possess sufficient capacity to store a lifetime's memories and convey these to God. More than this, it has to possess the capacity to store the records of previous lives,[6] and sufficient spare capacity to store all that we will be.

The information has to be arranged in an orderly manner so that God can read it, therefore it has to be filed, and the files have to be

---

6 Proof that the soul lives through many lifetimes is provided by people who, under hypnotic regression, have given detailed accounts of previous lives.
Clearly these people have opened files that God archived to the soul after scanning them. It may seem puzzling that God made these files accessible to us, albeit only under hypnosis, since they seem to be of use only to Him as a record of our progress since Creation. Moreover, if they became active during a subsequent lifetime, they would inevitably create a conflict of ideas and behaviour.
The reason God placed them at our disposal is that they contain information that will help us to progress. Those who have undergone hypnotic regression have thrown much light on the past. They have filled in many gaps in human history, and it is an old adage that "those who ignore history are condemned to repeat it."

registered in a directory that corresponds with the directory (and files) in the human mind. Consequently each time personality creates a file, a duplicate is created and registered in the soul; each time personality updates the file, the duplicate is updated.

The soul is therefore a back-up system, and it is a system that cannot be damaged because the soul, being ageless and intangible – not composed of flesh and blood – is unaffected by damage to the brain. Consequently when the mind is damaged and suffers memory-loss (amnesia), personality only has to copy the directory and files from the soul into an undamaged 'window' of the mind for it to be able to register new files (memories) and, as its thoughts open older files, remember what happened earlier.

We deduced that a procedure of this sort had to be carried out when we analysed amnesia, and the fact that we have arrived at the same procedure through our analysis of the soul proves the correctness of our analysis.

We should regard the soul as a computer that God designed, programmed and installed in each of us. It has processing powers far beyond those of the most modern computers, yet its nature is indeterminate. It is real but not material; invisible – because it has no mass – and undetectable, yet it contains the essence of our being. It gives an entirely new meaning to our likeness with God.

The soul contains every file and piece of information up to the moment of death. Since the soul is programmed to return to God at the end of each lifetime, He is certain to receive a complete account of our lives. Therefore at the moment of death the soul departs for Heaven.

Its departure shuts down the human brain.

* * * * * * *

Once the soul reaches Heaven, God scans its files. These were created by our ideas, plots, conspiracies and actions, hence God becomes aware of all our thoughts and deeds, both good and bad. Nothing is concealed from Him, and He can pronounce final judgement.

This has fearful implications for everyone who has harmed or abused another. Every criminal, murderer and terrorist will receive God's judgement and can expect to be punished. Every life they took thwarted His plan, because He requires each of us to live out the natural span of our lives.

In Revelation 20.12 it is written that the dead stand before God and are judged by the "book of life". Biblical scholars have interpreted this to mean the book provides the answers to those who plead justification for their actions, but this does not convey the full meaning and significance of the verse.

The meaning is that the dead are able to bear witness against the living! Many murder victims know the names or saw the faces of their killers. This knowledge was engraved on their memories and copied to their souls. When God scans their souls, He reads the names or sees the faces of their killers. He knows their crimes before they finally appear before Him.

The memories of victims constitute witness statements in the "book of life" that God can put to the accused as they try to justify their actions.

This adds a new dimension to the ability of the dead to act as silent witnesses. We have grown accustomed to the bodies of the departed yielding clues to forensic scientists, but now we have proved that their memories yield even more vital evidence to God!

Part 2

Prayer is a two-way form of communication – we ask God for help, and He responds – but no one has been able to explain where and how this form of communication was set up, how it works, and how prayers reach God.

We assume God is everywhere because we see and feel His power everywhere, but He can only be in one place at any given time. Yet God must have wanted us to pray to Him because it enables Him to take preventative action – to give us guidance, set us on the right path – instead of only being able to judge us at the end of our lives.

Therefore God must have installed the means whereby we can pray to Him anytime, anywhere. Since the soul is our link with God, it must contain a two-way link.

How does it work? The answer is to be found in the soul's computer programmes and processes. Prayers, like other thoughts, are electronic, hence prayers despatched from the soul equate to emails. These will reach God if we have His email address, and He will be able to reply if He can identify each caller. Therefore a programme in the soul must constitute an internet broadband facility.

God must have created this facility, then encrypted His email address and assigned to each of us a unique email screen name and address that are automatically attached to each prayer – a subliminal part of the message that only He can read.

The encryptions prevent the Devil from hacking into our emails and subverting people to his cause. Likewise God cannot use the facility to direct people's lives, because it is only activated when people turn to Him for advice and/or invite Him into their lives. God cannot override Man's free will.

Part 3

When we are mixing in society, we have to treat people with respect and courtesy. However, if an individual cuts himself off from society, and his character is no longer tested by the problems of normal everyday life, free will goes into overdrive. It tests the individual's character to the utmost, by forcing his personality to scan every human emotion and every type of sin.

This explains why members of the leisured classes, royalty and the aristocracy have, throughout history, exhibited a range of behaviour that the rest of society does not contemplate. It is no coincidence that sadism originated in the mind of the Marquis de Sade!

It is clear that after these people exited from the tests set by society, they were presented with tests from another source.

This can only mean God programmed free will to switch on automatically during our leisure hours and other periods of mental relaxation to ensure that every waking hour of every day our character is tested. We cannot opt out of the test of life.

Therefore those who retreat from the real world into a world of contemplation will be continually tempted. This particularly applies to those who have done so in order to worship God, such as monks and nuns of closed orders. It also applies, though to a lesser extent, to monks, nuns, friars and other religious persons who emerge from the houses of their Orders to busy themselves with good works in their communities.

It is an old adage that "the closer one gets to God, the more one is tempted," and now we know why!

No one was closer to God than Adam and Eve, and their lives were blissful – no toil, no pain, nothing to occupy their minds – so free will took control. It concentrated on persuading Adam and Eve to break the one command God had given them – not to eat the apple from the Tree of Knowledge – thus foreshadowing the temptation to break God's commands that constantly assails those in religious orders. This is yet another meaning behind God allowing the Devil access to Adam and Eve!

Chapter Three

The Fall From Grace of Adam and Eve

Part 1

According to Genesis 3.22, the sin that Adam and Eve committed was to eat "the apple from the forbidden tree of knowledge" before God had instilled in them His sense of righteousness. As a result, they had "become like God, to know good and evil," but had chosen of their own free will to become disciples of the Devil. He had, after all, persuaded Eve to eat the apple.

This episode is therefore an allegory that contrasts Devil-worship – paganism or idolatry – practised by prehistoric Man with the Garden of Eden, which represents the ideal state, a pure paradise because Man worships the one true God. One would therefore assume that, once Adam and Eve had succumbed to the Devil, God had no choice but to banish them.

However, this does not stand up to analysis. God needs us to understand the difference between good and evil, for how will we know the right way to live unless we have rejected the alternative? We develop our concepts, emotions and understanding through trial and error. God cannot programme us to master life.

We had to "eat the apple." It was a vital stage of our development, and the fact that we reached this stage through a sinister influence should not have resulted in banishment because, under God's influence, we would return to the right path.

God revealed the real reason for banishing Adam and Eve in Genesis 3.22. Once they had "become one of us, to know good and evil," they had to be prevented from eating the fruit of the tree of life, which God had planted "in the midst of the Garden", because then they would live forever.

Clearly the fruit represents 'something' that lives forever and elevates Man to a level at which he threatens God.

We believe this 'something' is Man's birth and rebirth together with his assertion of free will, as demonstrated by the disobedience of Adam and Eve, for it meant that Man, in each of his lifetimes, will evolve according to his own free will, and God will not be able to predict how he will evolve. After thousands of lifetimes, Man will be in Heaven, standing next to God, but he will be an unknown quantity. This is why God reacted to the possibility of Adam and Eve eating the fruit of the tree of life as if it was a direct threat to Him.

We have to bear in mind that God wished to exercise strict control over the number and qualities of Man, not have these factors determined by Man's free will. This is symbolised in Genesis by God creating Adam and then Eve, after realising Adam was not fit for purpose.

Part 2

The only means by which God could exercise strict control was to install in the soul programmes that develop a fertilised human egg into a mentally and physically co-ordinated human being. This logical extension of our theory conflicts with medical science, which says the programmes are encrypted in DNA because it is present at conception, shows the layout of the human body, including the place occupied by every cell, and determines our physical characteristics. However, DNA cannot instigate bodily rhythms and systems.

Scientists describe rhythms such as heartbeat, temperature, brain rhythms and peristalsis (motions in the alimentary canal that allow the passage of food) as 'automatic', meaning they have no apparent starter, but there is abundant evidence showing that people can control these functions. Psychologists Joseph Kamiya and Elmer Green discovered that if patients saw their brain rhythms on a screen, then they soon learned to control them. This means there is a mechanism or 'switch' that can adjust default settings, and it is located in the brain.

However, the brain does not develop until four weeks after the embryo has formed, and by then various other developments inside the embryo have taken place. Rudiments of the spinal cord and nervous system have formed, together with the eyes and ears. An S-shaped heart has begun pulsating and pumping blood; it also has separate chambers.

Therefore something else has to be present in the fertilised human egg, and this something contains the programmes that govern every stage of our development. It is also invisible and undetectable because it has no mass.

These considerations lead to only one conclusion: God wrote the programmes (because He created Man and has a complete understanding of his body) and installed them in the soul (because they can only be installed in a fully functioning control centre) which is invisible.

* * * * * * *

In due course the soul inserts itself inside the fully formed brain, but where does it reside? The cerebral cortex is divided into two symmetrical hemispheres. The right hemisphere is our seat of intuition and emotions, the left hemisphere deals with reality and the outside world. They are connected by a massive band of axons, the corpus callosum, whose function is to transfer information between the hemispheres. This information has to be passed to our personality, which therefore has to be connected to the axons. Personality is embedded in the soul, hence the soul has to install itself in the tiny gap that separates the hemispheres, and tap into the axons.

After this, the soul links up with the mind and the rest of the brain. It is thus linked to the central nervous system, which enables it to instigate and adjust bodily systems/rhythms. It is also linked to the thoughts, dreams and desires that flow from our mind, and this enables it to transcend its rôle as a computer and become our spiritual centre.

Part 3

God not only wished to ensure that we developed both physically and spiritually but that the same applied to our evolution – he forbade Adam and Eve (Man) from eating the fruit of the Tree of Life – hence the soul contains programmes that govern human evolution.

Evolution is the process that upgrades the programmes, systems and settings governing our physical and mental properties. The programmes equate to a computer's administration departments. These are housed in the computer's control centre, which is accessed through the My Computer window. The soul is a computer, hence a window of the soul is My Computer.

This window has to link up with the entire human brain, partly because devising and assessing the options for evolution means harnessing ideas from both hemispheres of the brain, but also because the information thus gathered has to be stored in our memory, alongside calculations showing adjustments to size, proportions and settings, so that a template of the new design - equivalent to an architect's drawings - can be created.

The template is no mere exercise in calculation, for it requires imagination to conceive the final form and bring it about. This means the source of evolution has to be highly intelligent, and we have only one such source: personality.

Personality is housed within the soul, hence it has access to the governing programmes, systems, devices and settings. Personality is also our equivalent of a computer-operated mouse, so it has the ability, facilities and intelligence to make whatever changes it feels are necessary.

When personality feels that change desirable or necessary, it generates thoughts that open the control centre. Using its programme of free will to think imaginatively, personality calculates the changes that have to be made, and draws up a template.

Every change entails a change to our genetic make-up. Some genes have to be switched off and others have to be rearranged and modified. Our genetic code is encrypted on a double helix of DNA, consequently evolution only begins after personality has calculated the changes that have to be made to DNA.

We will not benefit from these changes because we cannot change the programming – the DNA – in the billions of cells that make up our body. The beneficiaries are our offspring. We can alter their DNA because this only entails altering the programming in one cell. Our personality despatches hormones – chemical messengers – to our sperm or eggs. The hormones transfer the information detailing the changes to enzymes – biological catalysts that modify DNA – and these make the requisite changes.

This is the only logical explanation for the evolutionary process, but it rests on our theory of the human soul.

* * * * * * *

The soul is our spiritual centre, consequently the programmes and processes in the soul are intended not only to improve us physically and mentally but also to heighten our spiritual awareness.

Evolution takes place on all three levels. Physically it entails changes to bodily rhythms and systems that produce powers verging on the miraculous. Yogis or fakirs suspend their breathing until it is undetectable, whilst being buried alive for weeks at a time; display different pulse rates in each wrist; and walk on fire. US psychologists Elmer and Alice Green described the feats of Jack Schwartz, who withstood beating, burning and stabbing not only without pain but also without injury.

The soul aligns evolution with increasing spiritual awareness. Yogis hold their powers in low esteem because their main aim is to gain control over their bodies and emotions so that their minds move inward towards the 'source of power, meaning and purpose'. We agree that their 'miracles' have no religious significance because they result from adjustments to the body's rhythms and systems that equate to the adjustments operators make to computers to improve various aspects of their running. However, they do point to the 'source of power, meaning and purpose', inasmuch as the only mechanism that can adjust the body's programmes lies within the soul.

We can also align genetic modifications that God carried out on the brain with increased spiritual awareness. It is most apparent in the extraordinary feats of yogis during meditation. These were described by a French lawyer, Louis Jacolliot, who was in India during the early 1860s. In his *Occult Science in India*, Jacolliot says one fakir caused a pawpaw seed to sprout into an 8in. plant in two hours by meditating above it, whilst another caused a small table to stick to the floor so firmly that all Jacolliot's attempts to move it only succeeded in breaking it.

There is a link between achieving the relaxed state of mind necessary for meditation and modifications God made to the pineal gland. The link was formed after God upgraded the pineal to assist spiritual awareness and positioned it mid-brain, where the soul inserts itself. In this sense Dr. Chen and his colleagues were quite correct to regard the pineal as close to the soul.

Part 4

The soul is non-material and therefore does not age. Nor can it be destroyed by natural events or explosions. Consequently when Man's forerunners were obliterated by the Big Bang, their souls lived on. But they lived in limbo because they were bodiless. In due course God rectified this situation: He recreated Man.[7]

Therefore our souls are the souls of our forerunners who lived before the Big Bang. The link – the continuity – was essential, because they contain the knowledge, talents and skills necessary to recreate objects from God's blueprints. We play the same part in God's plan as they did, and we need their understanding.

This explains why we have innate patterns of behaviour and one or more talents - inherent knowledge and understanding of certain subjects. These are the hall-marks of intelligence, and means each of us is intelligent before we are born!

There is ample proof that early Man inherited advanced knowledge. Certain astronomical and scientific knowledge was known in the far past before the technical capacity for making such observations had been discovered. The Babylonians knew four of Jupiter's satellites and seven satellites of Saturn. Carved on a solid 10-ton gate standing on a 13,000-foot plateau at Tiahuanoco, Bolivia, is a system of designs dealing with the position of the Moon according to the time of day, together with indications of the equinoxes and solstices. The Moon's real and apparent movements are also shown, proving that the carvers were aware of the rotation of Earth.

Further proof of inherited knowledge is the mastery of mathematics by early civilisations, especially their ability to calculate enormous sums. The Babylonians resolved simultaneous equations, were familiar with the concept of zero, and dealt with enormous numbers - 15 to 20

7 Genesis 2.7 expressly states that after "God formed Man" he became "a living soul."

ciphers – using them to calculate dates and time periods on a cosmic scale.

On the opposite side of the world, the zero was in use in Mayan cities and observatories for thousands of years. The Mayas, or perhaps their predecessors, the Olmecs, came very close to calculating the exact length of the solar year, a measurement known only recently to our civilisation. The true measurement of the solar year is 365.2422 days, compared with the Mayas' 365.2420 days – an almost negligible difference.

This knowledge comes from such an early stage of cultural development that it could not have been slowly developed, and experts are convinced that races and nations began with it. This is consistent with our theory that Man inherited the knowledge of his highly advanced forerunners.

It is also consistent with Man's sudden appearance on Earth, as recounted in the story of Adam and Eve.

Who would have believed that an account in Genesis accords with the proof of inherited knowledge shown by these ancient civilisations?

CHAPTER FOUR
GOD'S COVENANTS

Part 1

AFTER THE FALL FROM grace of Adam and Eve, God drew up an agreement – the Adamic Covenant – that conditioned the life of fallen Man. One clause in the Covenant has turned out to be prophetic. It is given in Genesis 3.16, and changes the state of womanhood in two particulars: unrestricted conception ("I will greatly multiply thy conception"), and the headship of the man ("thy desire shall be to thy husband, and he shall rule over thee"). The entry of sin, which is disorder, necessitated a headship, and God vested it in the man (1 Timothy 2.11-14, Ephesians 5.22-25, 1 Corinthians 11.7-9).

However, God created Eve to represent *Homo sapiens*, a higher order than Adam (*Homo erectus*), hence the same must apply to women in general. Therefore God only conferred headship on men because the disorder was of a type that made the greater muscular strength of men of prime importance. God created such a disorder by removing His restriction on the growth of population, for tribes and nations expanded and came into conflict with one another.

This was the prelude to an event that occurred about 70,000 years ago, when *Homo sapiens*, in the shape of Neanderthal Man, abruptly disappeared, and the evidence suggests he was wiped out by a more highly advanced form of *Homo sapiens*, Cro-Magnon Man, the direct ancestor of modern Man.

We believe there is an oblique reference to this extinction in Genesis. Adam and Eve had eaten the fruit of the Tree of Knowledge of good and evil, and its seeds produced Cain ("acquisition") and Abel ("exhalation" or "that which ascends"). Cain is a mere man of the earth. His religion is destitute of any adequate sense of sin or need of atonement. Abel is a spiritual man. Cain offended God by refusing to bring Him a valid sin-offering – a sacrifice – and compounded the offence by murdering Abel.

Neanderthal Man likewise offended God, because evidence shows that he practised cannibalism, possibly for religious reasons, but nevertheless it was completely contrary to God's wishes (and to the later Christian communion service, in which the body and blood of Christ are symbolically consumed). Therefore Cain equates to Neanderthal Man, and his murder of Abel equates to the cannibalism of Neanderthal Man.

God punished Cain but allowed him to marry. Meanwhile Adam and Eve produced a third son, Seth, who was untainted by sin. His descendants are described in Genesis as "sons of God", and their inherent superiority over Cain (Neanderthal Man) means they equate to Cro-Magnon Man.

Genesis 6.2 says, "The sons of God saw the daughters of men that they were fair, and they took them wives of all which they chose." Research by UK psychologist Stan Gooch, shows that Cro-Magnon did not completely wipe out Neanderthal Man, because some Neanderthal females mated with Cro-Magnon males, hence the verse clearly refers to their intermarriage.

The same meaning can be applied to Genesis 6.4, which records that "there were giants in the earth in those days, and afterwards the sons of God came in unto the daughters of men, and they bare children to them, the same became mighty men." If we equate "giants in the earth" with Neanderthal Man, then the verse is another reference to the intermarriage between Neanderthal females and Cro-Magnon males.

Gooch went on to say that the intermarriage produced an exceptionally advanced race, which we equate with the "children" who "became mighty men", particularly as Gooch, noting that the offspring from the intermarriage were more intuitive and 'mystical', suggested they were the ancestors of the Jewish people.[8]However, the intermarriage between the descendants of Cain and Seth meant that Cain's failure to make a valid sin-offering to God was transferred to Seth's descendants. Thereupon God said, in Genesis 6.7, "I will destroy man whom I have created from the face of the earth."

Nevertheless, God spared Noah and his family, for reasons that become clear in later chapters of Genesis. Noah's eldest son, Shem, was a direct ancestor of Abraham, the first Jewish patriarch. In 2126 B.C., God told Abraham to go to Canaan, where He will make of Abraham "a great nation". This nation was Israel, and the Israelites were God's Chosen Race.

Likewise the intermarriage of Neanderthal females with Cro-Magnon Man would not have been enough to redeem Neanderthal Man in God's eyes, and the Flood equates to the extinction of Neanderthal Man. The Flood left only Noah and his family, who equate to Cro-Magnon Man infused by the finest Neanderthal qualities. The superior race that developed from the infusion equates to Shem's descendants, particularly Abraham, and ultimately to God's Chosen Race.

---

8 Professor Steven Mithen, of the archæological faculty at the University of Reading, also believes the intermarriage was the source of certain traits in the Jewish people, citing their extraordinary gift for music. The skeletons of Neanderthal Man show a high position of the larynx, suggesting they had high-pitched feminine voices that they used for singing. Professor Mithen believes the Neanderthals passed this to Cro-Magnon Man, who danced and sang to communicate complex emotions long before word-based language evolved. He also believes they may have developed an even more sophisticated sense of melody and rhythm than modern humans.

Part 2

Once we dismiss the idea that God flooded the world to ensure that only Noah and his family survived, then the Flood has to be regarded as an allegory for the washing away of Neanderthal Man's sins through the cleansing power of water. In this sense it was a precursor of baptism. However, Cro-Magnon Man had certain of the characteristics of Neanderthal Man, hence he had an irreducible element of unrighteousness, and this explains why God said, "I will not again curse the ground for man's sake; for the imagination of man's heart is evil from his youth" (Genesis 8.21).

It also explains why God drew up the Noahic Covenant that divided Noah's family (Cro-Magnon Man) hierarchically (Genesis 9.24-27): the descendants of Ham will be inferior and servile; from Japheth will descend the Gentile races; Shem will have a special relationship with God, and all divine revelation will be made through Semitic men.

This should be regarded as the literal truth, for God had the means of determining racial characteristics and endowing one race with superior qualities to play a more important part in His plan.

Each race evolves different physical characteristics and personalities. The soul governs evolution, and personality resides in the soul. Every soul is programmed to return to God at the end of each lifetime, giving God continuous access to them. Therefore God's ability to divide humanity into races results from His ability to infuse different qualities into souls.

* * * * * * *

The soul provides personality but chromosomes determine gender. It is, of course, essential to ensure that personality is compatible with gender, but this is not a problem because souls, during their many lifetimes, acquire personalities for both sexes. This is borne out by people who, under hypnotic regression, have given accounts of previous lives, in some of which they have been men, and in others women.

Therefore after the soul has overseen the development of the fertilised egg into a baby, it brings to the fore files containing the personality compatible with the baby's gender, and archives those pertaining to the opposite sex.

Souls not only have to be compatible with the gender of the baby but also bear the characteristics of the family into which it will be born. We are here referring not to physical characteristics, since these are passed directly by the parents to their offspring at conception, but to qualities of character. Since families have traits, and these could only result from the link up of family members with souls of compatible characters, there must be the means of ensuring that this is accomplished successfully.

Clearly every soul has to be arranged in Heaven in a particular order. Since souls contain character, and each character is different, this is a distinguishing factor. However, character is subjective and hard to define. A more precise alignment is needed.

Heaven divides into twelve sections that are defined by character and depicted by the signs of the zodiac. Each sign occupies a month in the calendar year. The similarity between the characteristics of a zodiacal sign and individuals born within its time-frame is so striking that it cannot be accidental or coincidental. There undoubtedly exists a close correlation between our date of birth and our character.

There has to be a reason for this alignment, and the only logical reason is that individuals born at a particular time are infused by souls of a certain character. Therefore souls must be arranged according to the signs of the zodiac.

However, this arrangement will only achieve compatibility if souls in Heaven know the exact time and date of conception. This information can be despatched by the mother's soul, for it can make use of the internet facility we described earlier to despatch an email to God the moment it is aware that conception has taken place. Emails automatically record time and date, and these allow God to know which souls to despatch.

Despatching a soul is equivalent to making an attachment to a reply email. Once the mother's soul has received the email, it can copy the soul (attachment) to the fertilised egg and delete the original. This is equivalent to the internet programme that allows attachments to be allocated to the appropriate files. The soul has no mass and therefore will not be rejected by the egg.

The procedures we have described are not only the most precise means of achieving compatibility and links, but also ensure that, after the death of an individual, the soul returns to the section of Heaven appropriate to its character.

* * * * * * *

The alignment endows a family with the general characteristics of their star-signs, but there will be specific variations due to a number of factors. Character varies within the same star-sign on a day-by-day basis. It also changes and develops during a lifetime, as it acquires experience and understanding. Since souls are ageless and live through countless lifetimes, the character embedded within each soul is continually changing. Individuals who are born at exactly the same time, but separated by one or more generations, will differ in certain respects from each other. Even twins, whose dates of birth may be only seconds apart, will have separate souls, each with a slightly different character. No two characters are exactly alike.

The arrangement does not lead to continuity or uniformity of character within a family, but this has many advantages. It enriches the family by giving its members the chance to possess talents no one within their circle has ever possessed. Moreover, members of the younger generation will eventually diverge from their parents' path and develop ideas of their own. This leads to progress.

*   *   *   *   *   *   *

The factors that determine a family's characteristics apply on a much larger scale, and give rise to races. This explains why God's designation of Shem's descendants as His Chosen Race was historically fulfilled. The Jewish people excel in the arts, sciences, and those professions particularly concerned with finance. Indeed, their achievements in the last-named field are so outstanding that they are synonymous with it. The same can be said of their success in the world of music. Less well known is the fact that five World Chess Champions have been of Jewish extraction, and many more have been leading contenders. All this, and we have yet to mention the towering figure of Albert Einstein – the greatest physicist the world has ever seen. It is no exaggeration to say that, from an intellectual standpoint, the descendants of Shem were in a class by themselves.

God must have genetically engineered their superiority so as to be certain that they could fulfil the special rôle He had in mind for them.

*   *   *   *   *   *   *

The necessity for such engineering becomes clear when we consider that God has to align our progress with His schedule (see *Introduction*). However, this presents no problems because He has continuous access to souls in Heaven. He can determine which soul to despatch when more than one soul has the same time and date of birth, and He can accelerate our progress whenever He feels the need to do so by despatching especially gifted souls. This would account for the sudden appearance of the geniuses that brought about the Renaissance.

Their appearance was not unheralded, however, for God uses planetary formations to announce significant infusions. Astrologers have noted that trines appear in the horoscopes of important individuals, and Grand Trines featured in the horoscopes of Rembrandt, Goethe and Leonardo da Vinci.

* * * * * * *

God's ability to determine the infusion of souls means we cannot fundamentally change the manner in which He dispersed Man across the globe. Therefore despite increased forms of intercontinental travel, races have preserved their distinct identities and strengths. This is why Brazilians continue to excel at football, Americans and Australians are ultra-competitive, and the Russians are masters of chess.

Even mixed-race marriages do not affect the dispersal pattern. DNA determines race, and the soul discovers the dominant racial genes after scanning the fertilised egg. It then adjusts its character and mindset to be compatible with race, gender and other genetic qualities.

Preserving racial and national identities seems to run counter to God's wish for us to achieve worldwide peace and harmony so that we can proceed to the next stage of His schedule, but the purpose becomes clear once we examine the differences between Eastern and Western mindsets.

The Chinese, Japanese and other Far-Eastern races, as well as the Hindus of India, are far more attuned to the mystical and spiritual aspects of life than Western races, which rely on pragmatism and calculation. This dichotomy reflects the differences between the right and left hemispheres of the human brain.

In the brain, the hemispheres have to be separated. If they were fused, the result would be indecision, muddled thinking, arguments, and a nervous breakdown. But we cannot achieve full understanding until the hemispheres are linked and communicating with one another. The same must therefore apply to mankind.

In the brain the soul provides the link, therefore mankind has to establish the same type of link by achieving pure spiritual understanding.

In doing so he achieves likeness with God. He also fulfils the essential precondition for the next stage of God's schedule.

Chapter Five
God's Message To Man

Part 1

According to Genesis 46.2-3, God said to Jacob, "Fear not to go down into Egypt, for I will go down with thee. There I will make of thee a great nation, and I will also bring thee back again."

However, the Egyptians would be bound to resist any attempt by the Israelites to develop into a great military force, therefore God must have intended them to acquire another form of strength.

The rôle God had assigned to the Israelites called for great spiritual strength, and it was this form of strength that God intended them to acquire in Egypt.

Where could the Israelites acquire such strength in Egypt?

The answer is: within the Great Pyramid of Giza.

Archæological excavations and scientific research have shown that the passages and chambers within the Great Pyramid replicate the oldest known work in literature, the *Book of the Master of the House of Hidden Places*. Both describe the same path for every individual who lives and dies, then reincarnates again and again to learn the lessons of life. The one tells the story in words, the other in stone.

Every Ego – the mental energy that makes up a personality – descends into incarnation from another plane, and as the incarnation begins – as the child takes its first breath – the Ego loses all conscious memory of its previous lifetime – it is in darkness. As one enters the Great Pyramid, it is on a descending angle. There is one hieroglyph inscribed in the limestone above the entrance – it is best translated as 'horizon of heaven'. This corresponds to the philosophy in the *Book of the Master*, for as each of us descends into life, so the horizon of heaven narrows and we are wrapped in darkness.

We invariably reach a point in our lives where we have to choose between elevating ourselves and beginning the ascending path that ultimately returns us to the Creator, or continuing the descent. However, the 'Gate of Ascent' is blocked – the elevation of one's character is difficult – so it is much easier to abandon the attempt and drift along a descending slant, remaining in the dark as to life's real purpose. Again this is allegorised in stone, for about sixty feet from the entrance, the ascending passage – the Gate of Ascent – leading upward into the heart of the Great Pyramid is blocked by three cubes of granite.

Egos that fail to pass through the Gate of Ascent continue to descend in darkness until they finally reach the 'chamber of upside downness', the chamber of 'chaos'. From here there appear to be various ways out, but they lead nowhere. Egos must therefore either die in darkness or climb all the way back to the Gate of Ascent and try again to achieve an upward path. However, all is not lost if they die in 'unknowingness', because they will be incarnated again and again until they choose to elevate. It is their choice.

In the Great Pyramid, after we reach the granite plugs that block the Gate of Ascent, we continue descending for more than 360 feet in confining total darkness until we reach a subterranean chamber. It had to be carved out of the rocky plateau, yet it is directly below the apex – another example of the perfect accuracy of the Great Pyramid's design.

The chamber translates 'chaos' into stone. The ceiling is dressed and relatively smooth, the floor is rough and unfinished – it is upside down. There is what appears to be another corridor, but it leads to a dead end.

A well shaft or corridor leads straight down, but it too is a dead end. This is chaos! A chamber built upside down and leading nowhere!

Egos in the 'chamber of upside downness' have to turn back, make their way to the Gate of Ascent, and choose whether to strive for human perfection. They do not know at this point that perfection is rejoining the Creator, but it is an inner urging that demands they elevate themselves.

They make their way through the Gate of Ascent and find themselves in the 'Hall of Truth in Darkness'. However, though they are on the right path, it is not easy – they must continue to make great efforts.

In the Great Pyramid, once beyond the granite plugs we still must practically crawl along because the passage is narrow and confining. It is also dark, but it does not become progressively darker, as in the descending passage, because we are moving upward and the passage corresponds to the Hall of Truth in Darkness.

Our physical life may expire at any point along the way, but we retain in our Egoic memory the lessons that brought us to this particular plateau of advancement, making it easier for us to choose the proper course when we are next incarnated. 'Girdle stones' indicate the various plateaux of advancement, and they are found every 17 feet 2 inches. This distance is also the dimension of the north-south floor in the two major chambers, both of which equate to key stages in Egoic advancement, as set out in the *Book of the Master*, hence the geometric symmetry is perfect.

As Egos work their way upward along the Hall of Truth in Darkness, they reach the 'Chamber of New Birth' or 'Second Birth', a major plateau of Egoic development. Here they can take stock of all they have learned during their ascent in darkness, and there will be a realisation of what they are struggling toward – a new awareness or consciousness of the reason for all the effort. In the Great Pyramid a corridor intersects the passage corresponding to the Hall of Truth in Darkness and leads to the Queen's Chamber, which therefore equates to the 'Chamber of New Birth'.

Egos armed with a new consciousness return to the ascending passage and emerge into the 'Hall of Truth in Light'. In the Great Pyramid we emerge into the Grand Gallery – a magnificent and spacious structure, filled with the promise of glory.

Every phrase or name for Egoic development in the *Book of the Master* perfectly fits the interior system of passages and chambers in the Great Pyramid.

The cleverness of the symbolism in the actual construction is shown by the necessity to crawl along the narrow ascending passage until we reach the Grand Gallery, when we can stand up and stretch our limbs. We can move upward easily in the huge, two-storey gallery. It is indeed the Hall of Truth in Light.

At the upper end of the Hall of Truth in Light is a great step that Egos have to climb before they can stand on a level floor. This is the floor of the temple. Egos are on the verge of what Buddhists and Hindus call 'liberation'. They have almost reached the pinnacle of this round of existence; once they pass through the 'Chamber of the Triple Veil' that stands before them, they need never again incarnate to the physical level – their Egoic growth will be completed on higher levels of existence.

The Chamber of the Triple Veil is obviously divided into three parts. According to the *Book of the Master*, the first part is 'inner conflict', the second part is 'truce in chaos', and the third part is 'final tribulation and humility'.

These divisions are exactly replicated in the construction of the Great Pyramid. At the upper end of the Grand Gallery is a great step of limestone, and once we climb onto it, we are standing on the floor of the main chamber, or King's Chamber. However, to enter, we must stoop down again and enter another cramped corridor. After the magnificent ascent in the Grand Gallery, we obviously hesitate before stooping and entering a narrow, confining corridor. This symbolises inner conflict.

We only crawl for a few feet in this first 'veil' and then we can stand up inside a small antechamber. We get a break in the confinement, and can reflect on our reaction to the confining entrance. We are also standing directly above the Chamber of Chaos, hundreds of feet below, and as we attune to this 'veil of truce', we can reflect on the millions of Egos who have yet to make the ascent.

Ahead lies the third veil, and once again we are forced to crouch to enter, but beyond this final low passage is the main chamber – the 'Hall of Judgement', the chamber of the 'open tomb'. It is with respect and true humility that we pass through the veil of tribulation and humility.

Once inside the Hall of Judgement, we are greeted by other evolved Egos. At the far end of the chamber sits a huge sarcophagus, but it is open and empty, signifying that, for us, death is no more. We have become immortal!

Every key portion of the philosophy in the *Book of the Master* is embodied in stone within the Great Pyramid, and together they define an inspiring individual philosophy.

* * * * * * *

Once we take into account the fact that God wished the Israelites to go to Egypt, had paved the way for them by insinuating Joseph, the youngest son of Jacob, into the position of key advisor to the Pharaoh, had given them a legitimate basis for entering Egypt by designating the western border of the land He had promised Abraham as "the river [Nile] in Egypt" (Genesis 15.8), and the Great Pyramid stands at the head of the Nile Delta, then it is clear that God knew the Great Pyramid contained a spiritual message for the Israelites and He was the author of the message.

We have thus solved the greatest mystery of the Great Pyramid – the name of its designer – for it can be none other than God Himself. This explains why Jeremiah, one of the most renowned prophets, said God "has set signs and wonders in the land of Egypt, even unto this day," and Isaiah spoke of an "altar to the Lord in the midst of the land of

Egypt," and also of "a pillar to the Lord at the border thereof." A chart of the Nile delta shows that it is neatly encompassed by a quadrant from the Great Pyramid, which is therefore situated at the border and in the midst of Egypt.

Even more remarkable is the fact that the *Book of the Master* and the allegories in stone match key aspects of our theory – the immortality of the human soul, countless reincarnations to learn the lessons of life, memories of previous lives archived to our soul – that we reached by completely different lines of reasoning, therefore our theory is validated by none other than God Himself!

Part 2

Many people who have spent a few hours alone in the main chamber have experienced a feeling of spiritual enlightenment. Guided by an unseen force, they have given way to profound introspection. Why am I here? Who am I? What am I? What progress have I made towards my ultimate goal? These experiences prove that the Great Pyramid not only embodies a spiritual message but also contains a spiritual force, and the King's Chamber is of special significance.

We believe it was in the King's Chamber that God intended to impart to the leaders of the Twelve Tribes of Israel the true meaning of their lives – to reveal the reason why the Israelites are His Chosen Race, the part they play in His plan, and the mission He has in mind for them.

However, God could not appear before them in His full glory because, as He told Moses, "thou canst not see my face and live" (Exodus 33.20). Therefore whenever He had to speak to someone directly, He resorted to descending in a cloud and speaking from its midst, as when He and Moses met on Mount Sinai to compile the Ten Commandments: "And Moses went up into the mount, and a cloud covered the mount.

And the glory of the Lord abode upon mount Sinai, and the cloud covered it six days; and the seventh day [God] called unto Moses out of the midst of the cloud. And the sight of the glory of [God] was like devouring fire on the top of the mount in the eyes of the children of Israel" (Exodus 24.15-17).

The necessity for God to descend to the King's Chamber in a cloud accounts for two features of the Great Pyramid's internal structure that have baffled pyramidologists. In the north and south walls of the chamber, at a height of about 3 feet above the floor, are the rectangular apertures of two shafts, the northern at an angle of 31° and the southern at an angle of 45°. Both lead to the outer surface and would appear to be ventilation shafts, but Egyptologists, assuming the Great Pyramid was built to house tombs, have been unable to explain why mummies would need ventilation. Dr. I. E. S. Edwards in *The Pyramids of Egypt* suggested they were intended for "some religious purpose," and this has given rise to the theory that they were the means by which the souls of dead Pharaohs ascended to Heaven. However, we have proved that God designed the Great Pyramid, therefore we have to find a reason why He would need these shafts.

The reason is that they provide the means by which He can descend in a cloud through the Great Pyramid to the King's Chamber and, after having spoken to the leaders, make the return journey back to Heaven.

* * * * * * *

It might be thought impossible to deduce what God would have said to the leaders, because He never had an opportunity to meet them on these terms – they never entered the Great Pyramid because the Pharaoh confined the Israelites to Goshen and his successor enslaved them – but the picture of God addressing the twelve leaders previews the scenes in which Jesus, the Son of God, addresses his twelve disciples, hence we should be able to infer God's words from those of Jesus.

CHAPTER SIX
JESUS' MESSAGE TO MAN

Part 1

OUR ANALYSIS SHOWS THAT Jesus incorporated a sub-text in his teachings that corresponds exactly with the philosophy that God incorporated in His design of the Great Pyramid.[9]

The sub-text has gone unnoticed because Jesus cleverly subsumed it into Christianity. For example, he encapsulated God's philosophy in his Sermon on the Mount, but broadened it to set out a code of conduct for Christians that biblical scholars have described as the divine constitution for righteous living.

There are two versions of the Sermon (Matthew 5-7 and Luke 6), but certain passages are common to both, and must represent the most accurate parts of the reports. From these passages we derive a number of themes.

The first is humility: "Blessed are the poor in spirit," wrote Matthew, "for their's is the kingdom of Heaven." This is repeated in Luke's version: "Blessed be ye poor; for your's is the kingdom of Heaven."

Therefore one must not be proud, which leads to another theme: do not seek earthly riches. "Lay not up for yourselves treasures on Earth...

9 This explains why Egyptian and Pyramid Messianic texts refer to the Messiah – Jesus – as Lord of the Pyramid.

but lay up for yourselves treasures in Heaven…No man can serve two masters, for either he will hate the one and love the other. Ye cannot serve God and mammon" – Matthew.

Similarly in Luke: "Woe unto you that are rich! Woe unto you that are full!"

The humble man does not sit in judgement upon others, particularly if he lacks righteousness as defined by Jesus, hence the next theme: judgement on others is forbidden. "Judge not, that ye be not judged" – Matthew. Likewise in Luke: "Judge not, and ye shall not be judged."

This leads to the next theme: forgiveness. "Blessed are the merciful" – Matthew. In Luke, the theme is repeated: "Be ye therefore merciful, as your Father is also merciful."

These themes foreshadow the next theme: pacifism. "Blessed are the meek, for they shall inherit the Earth…Ye have heard it said, 'An eye for an eye, and a tooth for a tooth,' but I say unto you that ye resist not evil. Whosoever smite thee on thy right cheek, turn to him the other. If any man sue thee at the law, and take away thy coat, let him have thy cloak also…Give to him that asketh, and to him that would borrow of thee, turn not away…Ye have heard it said that thou shalt love thy neighbour and hate thy enemy, but I say unto you, love your enemies" – Matthew.

These words are echoed in Luke's version: "Love your enemies, do good to them which hate you. Unto him that smiteth thee on one cheek, offer also the other; and him that taketh away thy cloak, forbid him not to take away thy coat also. Give to every man that asketh of thee, and of him that taketh away thy goods, ask not for them again."

Clearly Jesus believes victory is achieved by pacifism, but this means his followers will suffer at the hands of sinners, hence the next theme: suffer persecution. "Bless them that curse you, do good to them that hate you, pray for them that spitefully use you and persecute you. Blessed are ye when men shall revile you, and persecute you…for my sake. Rejoice and be exceedingly glad, for great is your reward in Heaven" – Matthew.

Similarly in Luke: "Bless them that curse you, and pray for them that spitefully use you."

The theme of pacifism provides another reason for the rejection of wealth, since it can lead to conflict. Thus: "If ye lend to them of whom ye hope to receive, what thanks have ye? For sinners do the same. But [if] ye lend to your enemies, hoping for nothing in return, then your reward shall be great. Ye shall be the children of the Highest" – Luke.

The themes of the Sermon are implicit in the philosophy God embodied in the Great Pyramid because they show that one must ascend – rise above – earthly desires to acquire spiritual/Egoic perfection. However, they only provide a valid code of conduct for people living in society if God punishes those who are arrogant, judgemental, commit acts of violence, and persecute others. Consequently Jesus continually stressed that God is the final arbiter of Man's conduct: "Be ye therefore perfect, even as your Father which is in heaven is perfect…For with what judgement ye judge, ye shall be judged" (Matthew). Similarly in Luke: "Condemn not, and ye shall not be condemned."

Therefore we have to appear before God to be judged, and this is consistent with Egos having to enter the Hall of Judgement. Jesus fills in the necessary details by explaining the proceedings in a parable in Luke 16.19-31. A rich man dies and is buried, but his soul goes to hell. A beggar named Lazarus also dies, but his soul goes to Heaven. Jesus explains that they suffered contrasting fates because the rich man gave no sustenance to Lazarus, even though he had been brought to the rich man's door in the hope that he would be allowed to eat the bits of food that fell from the rich man's table.

This parable was intended to show that God judges us by our actions. It is therefore consistent with the passage in Revelations 20.12 (to which we referred on p. 79) that says God judges us by the "book of life."

However, certain aspects of the parable do not appear to be consistent with reincarnation, which is the key to achieving Egoic perfection. Hell is derived from the Greek "hades", meaning "the unseen world", and is the place for departed human spirits between death and resurrection. Biblical passages in which hades occurs make it clear that, before Jesus' ascension, hades was divided into two regions, the abodes respectively of the saved and the lost. The former was called "paradise" or "Abraham's bosom" (a Talmudic designation that Jesus adopted). The blessed dead were with Abraham, they were conscious and were "comforted" (Luke 16.25). The lost were separated from the saved by a "great gulf fixed" (Luke 16.26). The representative of the lost in hades is the rich man. He is alive, conscious, in the full exercise of his faculties, memories, etc., but he is in torment.

The lost remain in this state until God passes Final Judgement, whereupon they are taken to the lake of fire (Revelation 20.13-14). This means that, throughout their time in hades, the lost were given no opportunity of showing God they could become righteous and worthy of being saved, yet in the Great Pyramid God clearly showed that Egos reincarnate, which gives them as many opportunities as they require to take the ascending path to righteousness.

This apparent contradiction can, however, easily be resolved. The lost in hades are databases that God copied from their souls onto CDs/memory sticks and keeps in storage. The storage facility constitutes the "book of life." Final Judgement is the incineration of CDs/memory sticks in respect of those who have not achieved spiritual perfection.

After God copied the information from the rich man's soul, He archived the databases to a 'window' of the soul, consequently when the soul begins a new life the rich man begins a new life. But he has not been reincarnated because he only exists in archived files. Meanwhile the soul acquires a new personality and new memories that revise, update and supersede the data – memories, moral and spiritual values – of its previous lives. This means it is the soul of the rich man, not the rich man himself, who is reincarnated, and in this sense Jesus was absolutely correct to say that the rich man must achieve spiritual perfection during his lifetime if he is to be remembered – saved – at Final Judgement.

This shows how deeply one has to analyse Jesus' words to arrive at their true meaning.

Part 2

The undeniable link between God's spiritual message in the Great Pyramid and Jesus' doctrine of Christianity means there is an undeniable link between God's failure to impart His message to the leaders of the Twelve Tribes of Israel and His decision to send His only son, Jesus, to minister to the Israelites.

To understand how both fitted into God's schedule, we have to examine Jesus' ministry.

Jesus changed the course of human history more profoundly than anyone before or since, therefore Man must have veered so far off schedule that God decided the only way to bring him back on course was through the power and authority of His son, Jesus. God's decision was vindicated, because Jesus only achieved the desired result by convincing his disciples and followers of his divine nature through the circumstances surrounding his birth, transfiguration, resurrection, and ascension.

No one, however, has been able to explain how Jesus came into this world because his mother, Mary, was a virgin when she gave birth. This has given rise to a fundamental doctrinal dispute concerning Jesus' origin. How could he be the Son of God when he did not have a divine mother? What was the relationship between the human and divine in Jesus? The life, death and resurrection of Jesus convinced many of his followers that Jesus was also God, but this would mean Father, Son and Holy Spirit were One. How are they related?

We shall answer all these questions – and many more – in this chapter.

*   *   *   *   *   *   *

Mary was a virgin[10] when she gave birth to Jesus, which meant Joseph had no input into Jesus' DNA, but Mary had been visited by an angel of the Lord prior to conception, as had her sister Elizabeth prior to giving birth after being declared barren, so the visitation by an angel is the common factor in these births.

People who believe they have been visited by an angel tell of feeling a superhuman strength of purpose through complete surrender of their will to that of a higher being. We may assume that the visits of an angel to Elizabeth and Mary had the same effect, for the angel Gabriel had told Mary that "The Holy Ghost shall come upon thee, and the power of the Highest shall overshadow thee" (Luke 1.35). The "overshadowing" would have enabled the angel to gain control of their personalities, instigate the evolutionary process that we described in *The Human Soul – 3* to bring about changes to the DNA in one of Elizabeth's and Mary's eggs, and then fulfil the rôles of the absent husbands by fertilising the eggs.

In both cases, but especially that of Jesus, who was of a higher order than Man, the changes had to be extraordinary, and only an extraordinary agency such as an angel could have made the necessary calculations.

10 It has been suggested that "virgin" is a mistranslation of *halmah*, which in the Old Testament means an unmarried girl of marriageable age, and presumed to be a virgin in the Jewish moral code. However, Gospel-writers Matthew and Luke clearly state that Mary was espoused to Joseph.

Some historians believe Nazareth was the more likely site for the birth of Jesus, but the Bible specifies Bethlehem. Joseph had to travel to Bethlehem because he belonged to the House of David (in I Samuel, 17.12 it is stated that "David was the son of Ephrathite of Bethlehem"), and both Matthew and Luke specify Bethlehem as the place where Mary gave birth. Furthermore, the descending passageway in the Great Pyramid points directly at Bethlehem, and the Great Pyramid is never wrong!

Elizabeth and Mary would have been in a trance-like state during the entire process, like subjects during sessions with hypnotists, and this accounts for their inability to remember or explain how they were able to conceive.

The angel Gabriel told Joseph that, although God had chosen his wife to give birth to Jesus, nevertheless Jesus was "of the Holy Ghost" (Matthew 1.20), meaning that Jesus and God were composed of the same material. This precluded an input of Mary's DNA, hence the angel had to remove Mary's DNA from the egg that it was about to fertilise.

Jesus' soul likewise had to be God-like, consequently God was able to set parameters in Jesus' soul that guided Him in determining the qualities and powers of Jesus' DNA. This explains why Jesus was able to perform miracles.

Upgrades of this magnitude confirm Jesus' status as the Son of God, and to remove any doubt on this point, God Himself confirmed that Jesus was His son on two occasions, the first after Jesus' baptism: "And lo, a voice from heaven saying, This is my beloved Son, in whom I am well pleased" – Matthew 3.16, Mark 1.11, Luke 3.22. Later God affirmed that Jesus was His son during Jesus' transfiguration.

The transfiguration is recorded in Matthew 17.2-8, Mark 9.2-8, and Luke 9.28-36, so there can be no doubt as to its authenticity. Matthew says, "Jesus was transfigured before Peter, James and his brother John. His face did shine as the sun, and his raiment was white as the light." Shortly afterwards, "a cloud overshadowed them, and a voice out of the cloud said, This is my beloved Son, in whom I am well pleased."[11]

---

11 Luke goes onto say, "when the voice was past, Jesus [who had been joined by Elias and Moses] was found alone." Mark also says the disciples, after hearing God's words, "looked round about, but saw only Jesus." This means "overshadowing" is a term for a trance-like state, and proves the correctness of our theory that Elizabeth and Mary would have been in such a state during the operations that the angel Gabriel performed on them.
The presence of God in a cloud is reminiscent of His "descending in a cloud" to Moses on Mount Sinai (Exodus 34.5). Jesus' radiance is reminiscent of the energy that God radiated and which had an extraordinary effect on Moses. Exodus 34.30 says, "When

These episodes prove Jesus was the Son of God, and disprove the belief amongst certain religions that Jesus was merely a prophet.

* * * * * * *

The event in Jesus' life that had the most far-reaching consequences was his resurrection. Many theories have been put forward to explain it, but none have been convincing. However, in the light of the deductions we gave earlier, the explanation is simple: Jesus' body suffered like that of a human being's during the crucifixion, for it was pierced by the nails that held it to the cross, but because it was composed of God-like material it would not decay like earthly tissue.[12] Like the soul, it was immortal.

In this sense Jesus' body and soul were conjoined.[13] This means Jesus was alive after he was taken down from the cross, because his soul was active and could maintain the body's rhythms and systems. However, it would have reduced their levels to the absolute minimum, and been undetectable to those who took him from the cross and laid him in the sepulchre. This is analogous to the feats of yogis who suspend their breathing until it is undetectable.

Since Jesus was dead yet alive, we can explain his appearance to Mary Magdelene at the sepulchre. This episode is only given in John's account of the resurrection (20.14-18), but it is plausible. When Mary

---

Aaron and all the children of Israel saw Moses [after he emerged from a meeting with God], behold, the skin of his face shone, and they were afraid to come near him." Moses therefore decided to wear a veil when relaying God's commandments but, having to speak with God again, he removed the veil and "When he came out, the children of Israel saw that the skin of Moses' face shone."

12 This explains why Jesus' body was unchanged when he suddenly appeared in the midst of his disciples after the resurrection. Eight days later he dispelled the doubts of Thomas, who had not been present on the previous occasion, by saying to him, "behold my hands; reach hither thy hand, and thrust it into my side…and Thomas said, My Lord" (John 20.24-29).

13 This explains St. Paul's description of the Resurrection in 1 Corinthians 15.42-4: "So also is the resurrection of the dead…It is sown in a natural body; it is raised in a spiritual body."

realised she was speaking to Jesus, he said: "Touch me not, for I am not yet ascended to my Father." This must mean his body was being sustained by immense nervous energy equivalent to an enormous output of electricity, and it would have had a harmful effect on Mary.

The most significant event in Jesus' life was also the most breathtaking: his ascension to Heaven. Every moment is described in Mark 16.19 (similarly in Luke 24.51) as follows: "So then after [Jesus] had spoken unto [his eleven disciples], he was received up into heaven, and sat on the right hand of God."

No one has been able to explain how Jesus ascended to Heaven, but our theory solves the puzzle. His time on Earth was over, the energy that had sustained him since the resurrection was exhausted, and his soul automatically ascended to Heaven. But because his body and soul were conjoined (see our analysis of his resurrection) it too ascended to Heaven.

Part 3

With these proofs of his divinity, Jesus filled his disciples with awe, but he reserved these displays for them alone. To instil the same degree of wonderment in the Israelites, he demonstrated miraculous powers of healing.

However, these demonstrations have to be viewed in the overall context of Jesus' mission, which was to restore Man to righteousness and align him with God's schedule, therefore Jesus only healed those who believed in him. He healed a centurion's servant after the centurion had said, "Lord, I am not worthy that thou shouldest come under my roof; but speak the word only, and my servant shall be healed" (Matthew 8.8), Peter's mother after he had become one of Jesus' disciples (Matthew 8.14-18), a daughter who had touched his garment, believing it would heal her, "Daughter, be of good comfort. Thy faith hath made thee whole" (Matthew 9.18-22), and the daughter of a mother whose faith moved Jesus to say, "O woman, great is thy faith! Be it unto thee even as thou wilt." With these words her daughter was healed (Matthew 15.21-28).

Jesus always described his healing as a cleansing or washing away of sins. Thus after healing a palsied man Jesus said, "Ye [now] know that the Son of man hath the power to forgive sins" (Matthew 9.6).

The power to forgive sins had been granted to the priesthood under the terms of the covenant God had drawn up with Moses, and initially Jesus acted within its terms. Thus he healed a leper after the latter had called him Lord and master, and then told the leper to observe the Mosaic covenant by saying, "shew thyself to the priest and offer the gift that Moses commanded" (Matthew 8.4). But Jesus had agreed with God the terms of a new covenant that offered undreamt-of benefits to all who followed him.

Jesus revealed the terms of this covenant to his disciples at the Last Supper. He blessed the bread, broke it into pieces and gave them to his disciples, saying, "This is my body." He then gave each a cup of wine he had blessed, saying, "This is my blood of the new testament, which is shed for many for the remission of sins" (Matthew 26.28).

In this context, "testament" means a covenant – a legal agreement. Therefore the bread equates to the body of a legal document, and the wine to the red wax on the cover of such a document that is impressed with a seal to signify its authenticity. The seal is Jesus' promise.

Sin is opposition to God, manifested by absence of righteousness and acts that violate or disobey the revealed will of God. The penalty for sin is death, commuted to a blood sacrifice. "Without the shedding of blood there is no remission" (Hebrews 9.22).

This explains why Jesus, under the terms of the covenant, agreed to shed his blood to secure forgiveness of the sins of the "many." Forgiveness and remission are in Scripture interchangeable. Remission means sending away, and forgiveness is to separate the sin from the sinner. By the "many" Jesus meant members of his fellowship – Christians.

It is only in the light of this preamble that we can understand why Jesus had to be crucified, for at the crucifixion the imagery Jesus had presented to his disciples at the Last Supper became the reality: blood from Jesus' wounds ran down parts of his body, and he cried out to God, "Father, forgive them for they know not what they do," which sealed the covenant.

Thus the full text of Jesus' covenant says the sin of the true believer – Christian – interrupted his fellowship – membership of Christianity – and is forgiven after he has confessed and been penalised, but only on the basis of Jesus' propitiating sacrifice (1 John 1.6-9, 2.2).

The full scope and meaning of Jesus' covenant only becomes clear, however, when we see how it supersedes and cancels earlier covenants between God and Israel. In these, blood sacrifices "covered" the sins of Israel but, until Jesus' death on the cross, did not "take away" these sins (Hebrews 10.4). God "passed over" these sins (Romans 3.25) in anticipation of Israel being "covered" by Jesus' sacrifice. "The believer in Christ is now, by grace, shrouded under so complete and blessed a righteousness that the [Mosaic Covenant] has neither fault nor diminution. This is...the righteousness of God by faith" (Bunyan).

It was Jesus' sacrifice, not Levitical sacrifices, that made at-one-ment with God. The Old Testament sacrifices enabled God to persist with a guilty people because eventually they would come under Jesus' covenant. To the offerer they were his confession and expression of faith; to God they were the "shadows" (Hebrews 10.1) of which Jesus was the reality.[14]

---

14 Jesus' covenant also changed the meaning and significance of baptism. Jesus said, "Except a man be born again, he cannot see the kingdom of God...Except a man be born [again] of water and of the Spirit, he cannot enter into the kingdom of God" (John 3.3,5). Water is necessary to wash away prebaptismal sin. The necessity for a new birth arises out of the incapacity of the natural man to "see" or "enter into" the kingdom of God. However gifted, moral or refined, the natural man is

Therefore the difference between human and divine forgiveness is that human forgiveness means the remission of penalty, whereas divine forgiveness follows the execution of penalty. Human forgiveness rests upon and results from having already been divinely forgiven. This principle is declared in Matthew 18.32-33 and Ephesians 4.32.

Note that under the terms of the covenant Jesus only forgives a believer's sins; his deeds are still subject to judgement (Matthew 12.36, Romans 14.10, Galatians 6.7, Ephesians 6.8, Colossians 3.24-25). The verdict will result in either a reward or loss of a reward, "but he himself shall be saved" because his sins have been atoned for and are "remembered no more forever" (Hebrews 10.17).

* * * * * * *

The terms of the covenant signified that Jesus became the forgiver of sins, a rôle that had hitherto been God's prerogative. This did not entail a diminution of God's status; instead it meant that after the ascension God elevated Jesus. He became God's equal.

More than this, he became infused with God – a distinct part of God's being – for shortly before he was about to ascend, Jesus told

---

absolutely blind to spiritual truth, and cannot enter the kingdom for he can neither obey, understand or please God (Mark 7.21-23, 1 Corinthians 2.14, Romans 8.7-8, Ephesians 2.3). The new birth is not a reformation of the old nature (Romans 6.6) but a creative act of the Holy Spirit (John 1.12-13, 2 Corinthians 5.17, Ephesians 2.10, 4.24). The condition of the new birth is faith in Jesus crucified (John 3.14-15, Galatians 3.24). Through the new birth the believer becomes a partaker of the divine nature and of the life of Jesus himself (Galatians 2.20, Colossians 1.27, 1 Peter 1.23-25, 2 Peter 1.4; 1 John 5.10-12).

One is reminded here of the new births or reincarnations of Egos as they make their way up the ascending passage in the Great Pyramid, and with our theory that the human soul lives through many lifetimes. With each incarnation Egos lose all conscious memory of previous lives, which equates to our theory that God archives our memories of previous lives to the soul and to Jesus' requirement for water to wash away prebatismal sin.

This is another example showing that Jesus incorporated every strand of God's philosophy into a sub-text of Christianity, and both are incorporated into our theory, which we reached by completely different lines of reasoning.

his disciples to "teach all nations, baptising them in the name of the Father, and of the Son, and of the Holy Ghost." By using "name" in the singular, Jesus affirmed that God is one but his personality has become threefold, indicated by relationship (Father and Son), mode of being (Spirit), and the different parts taken by the Godhead in manifestation and in the work of redemption, e.g. John 3.5-6 (Spirit), 16-17 (Father and Son). In Matthew 3.16-17, Mark 1.10-11, and Luke 3.21-22, the three persons are in manifestation together.

The conjunction in one name of the Trinity[15] affirms equality of the individual parts and oneness of substance.

* * * * * * *

After Jesus' ascension a change took place in hades. There was now a higher paradise that Paul calls "the third heaven" (2 Corinthians 12.1-4), meaning it is in the immediate presence of God. The righteous dead, "absent from the body, at home with God" await the last trumpet. When it is sounded they "shall be changed. They shall become incorruptible... immortal" (1 Corinthians 15.52-53).

The "third heaven" corresponds exactly with the Hall of Judgement in the Great Pyramid. Egos that enter the Hall have reached the final stage of Egoic development. Egos can only be judged by a divine being, hence God presides. Egos that pass this stage see the open, empty tomb signifying they have become immortal.

Egos in the Hall of Judgement correspond with the righteous dead "absent from the body" and with our concept of the human soul ascending through countless lifetimes until it finally attains the spiritual

15 The Trinity had already become manifest immediately after Jesus' baptism for, as recorded in Matthew 3.16-17 (also Mark 1.10-11, Luke 3.21-22), "the heavens were opened unto [Jesus], and he saw the Spirit of God descending like a dove, and alighting upon him." At the same moment, God's voice was heard confirming that Jesus was His son.

level that satisfies God. Every key portion of God's spiritual message in the Great Pyramid is embodied in Jesus and in our theory.

Part 4

Jesus chose twelve disciples. The number calls to mind the Twelve Tribes of Israel, so Jesus must have intended his disciples to form the nucleus of a new Israel that would better fulfil God's purpose than the old Israel under Jacob and Moses.

This explains why Jesus only preached to the Jews and, in Matthew 10.5-6, instructed his disciples "not to go into the way of the Gentiles… but rather go to the lost sheep of the house of Israel." However, following his crucifixion and resurrection, Jesus told his disciples they must become apostles and convey his words to Jews and Gentiles.

This two-stage process suggests that God, after speaking directly to the leaders of the Twelve Tribes, would have invested them with the powers Jesus conferred on his apostles – the power to heal, cleanse lepers, cast out demons, raise the dead (Matthew 10.1-8, Mark 6.7-13, Luke 9.1-6) and the power to speak in different tongues (Act 2.2-4) – and then have arranged for them to be despatched worldwide.

The disciples established headquarters in Jerusalem, therefore we may assume that is where the Israelites would have established their headquarters, after having first settled in the Promised Land.

It would have made no sense for God to impart His wisdom to only one race, so He must have wanted the Israelites to spread His words.

Spreading God's words, demonstrating divine powers, acting for the benefit of others, receiving in return warmth, gratitude and admiration, the Israelites would have constituted a benevolent élite, and we believe it was only because God expected them to fulfil this rôle that He awarded them the distinction of being His Chosen Race.

* * * * * * *

The Acts of the Apostles is also in two parts. In the first, Peter is the leading figure, Jerusalem is the centre, the first Christian church is established, and its ministry is to the Jews. In the second, Paul is prominent, a new centre is established at Antioch, and its ministry is chiefly to Gentiles.

The Acts concludes with Paul's earliest ministry in Rome, A.D. 65, but other apostles established Christian communities even further afield, including seven in Asia Minor. Later the apostles would Christianise Armenia and establish Christian minorities in the Persian Empire, India, and amongst the Germanic peoples on the northern borders.

The apostles proved the correctness of God's belief that His Chosen Race could become a human highway of knowledge, and the entire operation was in keeping with God's strategy: to inculcate the Israelites, who would then convey His words to the rest of the world.

Jesus therefore not only delivered God's spiritual message but also ensured that it would be spread worldwide in the way God had originally intended.

* * * * * * *

The most remarkable achievement of the apostles and other Christians was to convert the majority population of the Roman Empire by the beginning of the fourth century. There were many reasons for this success. The apostles proved by repeated demonstrations of healing, casting out of demons and raising the dead, that they derived their powers from God. They also impressed on people the benefits of Christian fellowship, particularly the covenant with Jesus. Others might confess and be forgiven, but they would not receive God's forgiveness.

Christians thus stressed their privileges and exclusivity, but membership was open to all. This was an irresistible lure to the Romans, particularly as they had lost faith in their pagan gods and their Greco-Roman culture was crumbling.

The uncompromising stance of Christians, coupled with their

high moral nature and adherence to their convictions to the point of martyrdom also greatly impressed, but the key factor was the conversion to Christianity of the emperor Constantine and his successors. This guaranteed that the Roman Empire would adopt Christianity.

The importance of this achievement can hardly be overstated because it amounted to converting the known world, yet all the factors we have mentioned stemmed ultimately from Jesus. He had made the covenant, ensured the apostles had the necessary powers, preached to all classes of Jews – he did not treat women as second-rate, nor did he exclude children from entry into his church[16] – and instructed his apostles to do the same for Gentiles.

Part 5

To consolidate and increase its gains, as well as to endure "till time shall be no more," Christianity had to be capable of adapting to social, economic and political changes. It therefore needed a church and priesthood with the authority to update Jesus' teachings, and Jesus knew this. At his very first meeting with Simon of Jona, Jesus said to him, "Thou shalt be called Cephas (Peter)" (John 1.42), and the symbolism of this prophecy was later revealed at Cæsarea Philippi when, as a reward for Peter's profession of faith in Jesus as "the Son of the living God," he was told: "Thou art Peter, and upon this rock I will build my church. The gates of hell shall not prevail against it, and I will give thee the keys of the kingdom of Heaven" (Matthew 16.16-19). In other words, Simon had received a new name that meant 'Rock' to indicate his place within the church.

Roman Catholic teaching maintains that the extract, and especially

16 Christians equate baptism, which washes away previous sins, with Jesus saying, "Except ye be converted, and become as little children, ye shall not enter into the kingdom of heaven" (Matthew 18.3), and therefore allow infants to be baptised.

the reference to "the keys of the kingdom of Heaven," indicate the conferring of jurisdictional power upon Peter that, because the church is to last till the end of time, was to be transmitted to his successors. Even Peter's triple denial of Jesus did not deprive him of his privileged position, because after the resurrection he was given the opportunity of affirming his devotion to Jesus, and heard the reply: "Feed my lambs… Feed my lambs…Feed my sheep" (John 21.15-17).

This provided the basis for the founding of St. Peter's Church at Rome and the papacy with its established rules of succession. The papacy had the authority to define the Christian position on theological issues that threatened division within the ranks. Successive popes had the authority to redefine previous rulings. The papacy could thus adapt Christianity to changing needs and times. It could also redefine the rôle of the Church.

This is seen in the extent to which the Church adapted to the needs of mediæval times. Kings, princes and the nobility of Europe were followers of Christianity, and accepted the pope as their intermediary with God. This endowed the papacy with great power, and with this power came great wealth. The Church became so wealthy that monarchs turned to it for loans, and the Church adapted itself to become the basis for the banking industry.

Churches and temples were natural repositories for people's savings, because robbers feared angering God by stealing money from His Church. Priests thus became bankers, and the money deposited with them was recycled in the form of loans to rulers. The Church did not charge interest on these loans. Instead it seized the property of defaulters, which helped to make it the largest landlord in mediæval Europe. This more than covered its costs, so the Church justified its adaptations on the grounds that they would enable it to perform God's work "till the end of time."

However, its policies appeared to fly in the face of Jesus' teachings. In Matthew 6.19-21, Jesus had said: "Lay not up for yourselves treasures upon Earth…but lay up for yourselves treasures in Heaven…For where your treasure is, there will your heart be also." Later, in a conversation with a rich young ruler, Jesus said: "If thou wilt be perfect, go and sell that thou hast and give to the poor. Then come and follow me, for thou shalt have treasure in Heaven." The young man, after hearing those words, went away in sorrow, for he could not bear to part with his possessions. Jesus turned to his disciples and said: "Verily I say unto you, it is easier for a camel to go through the eye of a needle, than for a rich man to enter the kingdom of God" (Matthew 19.21-24). Finally, Jesus went into the temple of Jerusalem "and cast out all them that sold and bought. He overthrew the tables of the moneychangers and said unto them: 'It is written [in Isaiah 56.7] that [God's] House shall be the house of prayer, but you have made it a den of thieves" (Matthew 21.12).

This appeared to be outright condemnation of the acquisition of wealth and practices such as the charging of interest that underpin the banking system, but closer study shows that Jesus was condemning the perception of wealth as an end in itself, and the conversion of temples/churches into commercial/money-making enterprises. Neither of these strictures could have been intended to prevent the growth of banking and other financial institutions that serve the good of the community, hence Christians felt justified in gradually developing the financial institutions that have enabled the West to flourish.

The Renaissance was crucial for the development of the modern banking system, because it led to the Age of Exploration in the 16th and 17th centuries, the Age of Enlightenment in the 18th century, and the Industrial Revolution of the 18th and 19th centuries. During these periods, the wealth brought back from the Americas enormously increased the economy of Europe and the population increased. This necessitated a transformation of industry and agriculture, which could only be paid for by new forms of funding. Private banks became widespread, banking and monetary systems became ever more flexible and sophisticated. Interest-bearing debt gradually became the main form of financial industrial investment. Today it underpins production and construction companies, as well as retail businesses that cater for the mass consumption of manufactured goods.

* * * * * * *

These developments were so natural and necessary that they did not create a clash with Christian values, but they did bring about political developments that ended the mediæval subservience of the state to the papacy. It therefore became necessary to redefine the relationship between Church and state.

Jesus had dealt with this relationship when certain people, at the instigation of the Pharisees, asked him whether it was lawful for them, as members of a religion, to pay taxes to Cæsar, the Roman emperor. Jesus replied, "Render unto Cæsar the things that are Cæsar's, and unto God the things that are Gods."

Jesus' reply is quoted in Matthew (22.21), Mark (12.17) and Luke (20.25), so there can be no doubt as to accuracy, but what does it mean?

Clearly Jesus believed that Church and State could coexist without compromising their vital interests. However, this could only be achieved if each had something vital to offer the other. The State could provide the Church with security, but what could the Church provide the State that was of equal value?

The answer derives from the very nature of Jesus. He was the Son of God, therefore the Church was a direct link with God, hence the ruler of a state that won the approval of the Church could claim to have been appointed by God, and this would safeguard his position against rival claimants.

To give substance to the link between the Church and God, Christians adopted the Jewish custom of anointing grease or oil for medicinal purposes and applied it to Jesus.[17] He became the Lord's Anointed, a spiritual meaning that Paul expounded and expanded in his epistles. Jesus was also given the title Christ, which is derived from the Greek term Khristos, meaning 'the anointed one'.

Christians believe Jesus is 'the anointed one' – the Messiah – referred to in various biblical verses such as Psalms 2.2 and Daniel 7.13, 9.25-26. According to the Jewish Bible, whenever someone was anointed with the specific Holy anointing oil formula and ceremony described in Exodus 30.22-25, the Spirit of God came upon this person to qualify him or her for a God-given task. According to the New Testament, Jesus is this Anointed One (John 1.41, Acts 9.22, 17.203, 18.5,28).

The kings of the Old Testament were anointed with oil and only afterwards did they receive power through the Holy Spirit that came upon them. Jesus, on the other hand, was anointed because the Holy Spirit had come upon him during his baptism (Acts 10.38). Jesus was the power of anointment. God confirmed that Jesus was His Son both after the baptism and during the transfiguration, hence Jesus was the anointed of God.

Thus the difference between the power that the kings of Israel possessed and the power Jesus (The King of Israel) possessed is that a human high priest anointed the former but God Himself anointed Jesus.

The Church quickly realised that it could exploit the difference to become indispensable to the monarchies that emerged all over Europe after the collapse of the Roman Empire. Monarchy is one-man rule, hence the monarch has to have a greater claim to the throne than his/her rivals. The monarch therefore needed the approval of the Church,

17 Sick people were anointed in the name of Jesus so that they could be healed, e.g., "And [the disciples] cast out many devils, and anointed with oil many that were sick, and healed them" (Mark 6.13). "Is any sick among you? Let him call for the elders of the church; and let them pray over him, anointing him with oil in the name of the Lord. And the prayer of faith shall save the sick, and the Lord shall raise him up; and if he hath committed sins, they shall be forgiven" (James 5.14-15).

especially as the Church agreed to anoint the monarch during the coronation ceremony, thus giving God's seal of approval.

In Europe the Carolingian dynasty was the first to have anointed kings. In the seventh century, the coronation ceremony was rewritten to epitomise the Church's conferring a religious sanction of the monarch's divine right to rule. Sometime later, English and Scottish monarchies, in common with the French, included anointing in the coronation ritual.

However, anointing did not symbolise subordination to religious authority, hence it was not usually performed in Catholic monarchies by the pope but reserved for the (arch)bishop of a major diocese in the nation, consequently tension between Church and State inevitably arose because the ultimate loyalty of Christians is to Jesus and God, and they would feel compelled to disobey laws of a state that contravened the teachings of Jesus. In that event, they would constitute a threat to the security of the state, and would be persecuted or killed.

This difficulty confronted early Christian communities in the pagan Roman Empire, and they struggled to survive. However, they not only survived but also thrived, and Christianity became the dominant religion of the Empire.

The factor that inspired the early Christians was Jesus' crucifixion and resurrection, for it created an inextricable link between death and a place in Heaven. It meant that as long as Christians remained true to the faith, their earthly trials and tribulations were of no significance because they would receive inestimable rewards in Heaven. Christians were thus imbued with such strength of faith that no amount of persecution could weaken it. The number of Christians swelled to such an extent that, by the fourth century, the Roman Empire was virtually Christianised.

The Romans discovered too late that the apparent passivity of Jesus' "Love your enemies" was in reality a strategy that had induced them to overreact. By making martyrs of Christians, they unwittingly helped to increase the numbers of those drawn to the faith, until Christianity became irresistible.

This was the victory that propelled Christianity into the forefront of religions, a place it has occupied ever since. It was therefore a crucial result with regard to the fulfilment of God's schedule. Given that Jesus knew the details of God's schedule, we may assume he foresaw the outcome as he lay dying on the cross. It has a degree of inevitability that enables us to lay down a fundamental principle: "Love your enemies" means they will eventually become your followers.

However, Jesus saw even further ahead, because he provided the solution to another problem between Church and State. Church law and state law spring from two different sources, and therefore embody two different concepts of justice. Consequently, even when they legislate for the same offence, they prescribe different punishments. Since justice can only flow from one source, either canon (church) law or state law had to concede.

Jesus could not compromise on his beliefs, and he inspired in his followers the same strength of conviction, but he also showed, by his refusal to head an army, that his followers must avoid a military clash with authority, hence he must have believed that Christians could convert states without the use of force.

Jesus' judgement was proved correct because in the fifth century Christianity, without raising an army, became the official religion of the Roman Empire, and by the latter half of the Middle Ages every state in Europe had, without a struggle, infused Christianity into their laws. Neither side had compromised on vital principles, though for reasons of state security, statute law had to be the final authority.

Part 6

No human being could have inspired such devotion in his followers that they made Christianity the foremost religion in the short space of time allowed by God's schedule. There is, however, reason to believe God considered David (c. 1040-970 B.C.) to be a suitable candidate, for his life foreshadowed that of Jesus.

Both were chosen by God[18]; both were born in Bethlehem; David was a shepherd when Samuel found him, Jesus was referred to as The Good Shepherd; the five stones that David chose to slay Goliath foretell the Five Holy (or Sacred) Wounds that Jesus suffered during crucifixion; David was betrayed by his trusted counsellor Achitopel, and Jesus was betrayed by Judas, one of his most trusted disciples.

However, David committed a great sin – he impregnated Bathsheba, the wife of Uriah the Hittite, and subsequently arranged for Uriah to be killed on a battlefield – and God had to punish him. This must have convinced God that no man could provide Christianity with the leadership it required.

Thus God had a thousand years in which to pave the way for Jesus' introduction to Man, and this explains why every detail of Christianity had been worked out before Jesus began his ministry. His first sermon – the Sermon on the Mount – was a complete survey of Christian doctrine, and during subsequent teachings he neither added to it nor detracted from it. He had prepared answers to every question from his disciples, followers and sceptics. He foresaw the necessity for a church,

18 After God withdrew his favour from Saul, He told the prophet Samuel, "I will send thee to Jesse, the Bethlehemite, for I have provided a king among his sons...And Jesse made seven of his sons to pass before Samuel. And Samuel said unto Jesse, The Lord hath not chosen these. And Samuel said unto Jesse, Are here all thy children? And he said, There remaineth yet the youngest...And Samuel said under Jesse, fetch him...and he brought him in...And the Lord said, Arise, anoint him; for this is he. Then Samuel took the horn of oil, and anointed him...and the Spirit of the Lord came upon David from that day forward" (I. Samuel 16.1, 10-13).

and had solutions to the main sources of tension between Church and State.

Jesus must have agreed the terms of his covenant with God before he arrived on Earth, hence they must have also agreed to his crucifixion and resurrection. This explains why Jesus said in Matthew 16.21 (also Mark 8.31-38, Luke 9.22-27) that he "must go to Jerusalem and suffer many things of the elders and chief priests and scribes, and be killed, and be raised again on the third day". To emphasise the point, Jesus repeated the message to his disciples in Matthew 20.17-19, Mark 10.32-34, and Luke 18.31-34.

* * * * * * *

Only Jesus could have suffered crucifixion and, despite the agony, asked God to forgive us, because it is not a human reaction. It proves Jesus had a completely different mindset from that of Man.

The crucifixion was the seal on the covenant, so Jesus must have known his fate from the outset, yet he made no attempt to avoid it. He knew that he had to inspire his disciples, and he did so in ways that were beyond human understanding – his transfiguration, resurrection and ascension, combined with demonstrations of miraculous healing powers – and in ways that showed the noblest human qualities – unrivalled strength of conviction, fearlessness in the face of certain death, unheard of sympathy and understanding towards the weak and the poor.

Jesus provided the example his disciples needed, for they would become apostles and have to convert the rest of the world.

No man could have provided such an example.

* * * * * * *

Jesus used persuasion, not compulsion. He needed disciples, but laid down such stern requirements – all who followed him had to abandon everything – that he left the decision to the individual. He did not urge him to accept. The disciples took this as their cue to forego imposing

Jewish customs on Gentiles. When it was suggested, during a council in Jerusalem A.D. 52, that Gentiles had to be circumcised and observe the laws of Moses, the apostles rejected the idea, and wrote to Gentiles in Antioch, Syria and Cilicia saying, "We gave no such commandment" (Acts 15.24). This established the principle that Gentiles were not subject to Jewish law.

Christianity was thus able to adapt to the customs of other nations in ways that Judaism could not. It also seamlessly subsumed pagan rituals by Christianising them. This degree of adaptability combined with an outward-looking and politically sophisticated church authority meant Christianity could cope with the ever-changing social, economic, financial and political worlds in ways that other religions could not.

Jesus' presented his disciples and followers with a ready-made and coherent religion that answered all their needs and all their questions. Add to this Jesus' proof that he was the Son of God, and everything was in place for Christians to sweep all before them, exactly as God intended.

CHAPTER SEVEN
THE CHRONOLOGY OF GOD'S SCHEDULE

Part 1

THE INTERIOR OF THE Great Pyramid consists of an ascending tunnel intersected at various junctures by passages and chambers. The intersections align exactly with the positions of certain stars at particular times, thus creating a time-line or chronograph.

The time-line is delineated by extending the border between the north and west faces to a point below the surface where it is joined by a downward projection of the passage that ascends through the Great Pyramid. Where these meet is 6,000 pyramid inches (the 'pyramidal inch' = 1.0011 inches[19]) from the only physical marker in the entire structure – a granite slab affixed to the antechamber of the King's

19 Sir Flinders Petrie, the father of modern archæology, dismissed the idea of the 'pyramidal inch', but David Davidson, in the third edition of *The Great Pyramid – Its Divine Message*, co-authored with Bible scholar H. Aldersmith, pointed out a fundamental flaw in Petrie's measurements. Although Petrie had noted the hollowing-in of the Great Pyramid's faces, he had failed to extend this factor to the missing casing stones around the Great Pyramid's base. Had he done so, he would have found that the base length fitted the 'sacred cubit' of 25 pyramid-inches that Piazza Smyth had earlier asserted was the basic unit of measure used by the pyramid builders (see p. 160).

Chamber. Thus we have a straight line on which the chronological graph can be placed – a pyramidal inch-year scale covering 6,000 years. Each year consists of 365.242 days, because this is the number of days in a solar year indicated by the sum of the base sides of the pyramid.

The starting-date is arrived at by a combination of astronomy and the pyramid structure. It is 3999 B.C. at midnight of the autumnal equinox (22nd September). The entrance passage of the Great Pyramid descends according to geometric calculations and in line with the northern pole star – Alpha Draconis – on a cyclical basis of 1,290 years. Star charts show that this star shone directly down the passage at the autumnal equinox for a few years. The median year was 2144 B.C. Confirmation of this is provided by double-scored line on all four walls thirty feet down the passage, because they point directly to an important star – Alcyone, in the constellation Pleiades – at precisely midnight, autumnal equinox 2144 B.C. By measuring the downward projection of the passage in pyramid inches/years, we arrive at our starting-date of 3999 B.C.

This is five years before the starting-date Archbishop Ussher assigned to Genesis, but the difference only arises because Ussher was uncertain as to the duration of Deuteronomy. Once we take into account the fact that God designed the Great Pyramid to embody His spiritual message for the Israelites, then it is clear that He must also have set the starting-date for the time-line, which should have been the starting-date for Genesis, and Ussher made a mistake.

Thus there can be no doubt that the Great Pyramid monumentalises the chronology of God's schedule.

Part 2

Inch by inch, year by year, the time-line moves upward from the starting-date. A juncture is reached with the descending passage and the Gate of Ascent. The date, according to the time-line is 1486 B.C., which Davidson and Aldersmith proved is the exact date of the Exodus.

The next juncture is where the time-line intersects with the floor level of the Chamber of Second Birth, or New Birth. The floor level suddenly 'drops' a couple of feet for no apparent structural reason. But there is a reason, and it is truly remarkable. The floor line of the chamber strikes the ascending passage at 4th October 4 B.C., hence the New Birth refers to that of Jesus, Son of God.

One's first thought on reading this is that the Great Pyramid must be wrong, because Jesus was born on zero A.D. However, when Dionysius Eziguus compiled the Gregorian calendar we use today, he calculated that the birth of Jesus took place in the twenty-eighth year of the reign of Augustus Caesar, overlooking the fact that Augustus had ruled Rome for four years under his true name of Octavian. Therefore Dionysius made a four-year mistake. That Jesus was born on 4th October is open to debate, but, as we shall discover, the Great Pyramid is never wrong!

This is borne out by the fact that the Great Pyramid gives us the precise date for the crucifixion of Jesus. Exactly 33½ pyramid inches further up our chronograph from the previous intersection, the passage opens brilliantly into the Grand Gallery or Hall of Truth in Light. The date is Thursday 6th April, A. D. 30.

Again this raises a question mark, because everyone knows that Jesus was crucified on Good Friday, which would have been 7th April. But once again the Great Pyramid knows best! This was proved in 1973, when a professor from the University of Tennessee used a computer to work moon cycles back in time, and determined that the crucifixion actually took place on the date specified by the Great Pyramid!

This is truly astonishing forecasting, because it was made thousands of years before the event occurred. It could only have originated from God, because He alone had the authority to send Jesus to live amongst Man.

The Great Pyramid monumentalises God's schedule, and the fact that it only allocates 33½ years to Jesus' life on Earth enables us to explain one of the great mysteries of his last days: why he made no attempt to prolong his stay by avoiding arrest or defending himself at his trial. It also explains Jesus' words in the Garden of Gethsemane immediately before his arrest, when he prayed to God, saying, "O my Father, if it be possible, let this cup pass from me: nevertheless, not as I will, but as thou wilt."

This is the first time the true meaning of these words has been revealed.

Part 3

The Exodus and the life of Jesus are the only events singled out for inclusion in God's schedule until the time-line, continuing up the floor of the Grand Gallery, strikes the centre of the granite slab affixed to the antechamber of the King's Chamber.[20] It is 6,000 pyramid inches/years from the starting-point, and the date is midnight 22nd September 2001.

At this point the scale of the time-line changes so that it can focus on the twentieth century. Instead of each pyramid inch equalling 365.242 days, they now equal thirty days. The starting-point in the structure is the 'Floor of the Temple' facing the 'Chamber of the Triple Veil', more

20 This bears out our theory that God designed the Great Pyramid, because He would obviously wish to highlight the Exodus and the mission that Jesus undertook. Nor can it be coincidental that it is possible to project a line from the Great Pyramid directly to Bethlehem, the birthplace of Jesus, through the area of the Reed Sea where Moses parted the waters, and the angle of the projected line is the precise angle of the descending passage in the Great Pyramid.

commonly known as the King's Chamber. We reach the starting-date by ascending from the foot of the Great Step to its top. The date is 2nd August 1909. From this point and date we move forward, counting each pyramid inch as thirty days.

The first veil is 'Conflict'. The intersection of the stone marking at the beginning of the veil with our floor chronograph gives the date 5th August 1914, and the intersection of the stone marking at the end of the veil with our floor chronograph gives the date 11th November 1918. These mark precisely the beginning and end of the First World War.

The next veil is 'Truce in Chaos', which extended from the end of the War until 29th May 1928. On this date the granite block marking the beginning of the final veil – 'Tribulation and Humility' – intersects with our scale. Our tribulation was evidently to be of an economic nature, because on 29th May 1928, commodity prices on the London market began to decline. This caused a fall in the value of the pound sterling and began a hopeless battle to maintain the gold standard.

We reach a clear-cut perpendicular to the thirty-inch-day scale as we exit the room against the south wall of the King's Chamber. At this point we have to make a 90° turn to continue onward. The date is 20th August 1953. It was the day Russian scientists exploded their first H-bomb, which could have triggered a nuclear war with the USA and brought about the end of mankind, but it was also the day on which Earth entered the Age of Aquarius – a period of harmony and understanding.

Part 3

The time-line covers 6,000 years of human history. During this period anything could have happened, yet events unfolded exactly as God predicted. How was this possible?

God installed a wide range of checks and balances in our minds and souls, but none of these would have allowed Him to predict the course of history unless He could also predict the effect of Man's free will.

This ought to be impossible, however, because it entailed placing an exact mathematical value on an unknown quantity – the human X factor – yet there is evidence to show that God achieved the impossible and, not surprisingly, the evidence is in the Great Pyramid. It is the Great Pyramid's Displacement Factor.

Davidson discovered that the perimeter of the Great Pyramid fell short of perfection by 286.1022 pyramid inches, and he termed this figure the Displacement Factor. He then found that the factor was embodied throughout the Great Pyramid's structure. The interior passage system is offset to the left of the north-south axis by exactly 286.1022 pd. inches. The centre of the King's Chamber is offset from the east-west axis of the monument by exactly 286.1022 pd. inches. Davidson claimed the missing apex was short from the projected point by exactly 286.1022 pd. inches. The precise difference in the height of the ascending passage and the height of the Grand Gallery is 286.1022 pd. inches. The figure is repeatedly embodied in the construction of the Great Pyramid and this must have been deliberate, because everything else in its construction is mathematically perfect.

The Displacement Factor is an amazing number. Davidson pointed out that it has many scientific uses – from determining the rate of precession to a theory of relativity.

Davidson believed the factor showed that "the builders did not carry out the precise intentions of the designer." Since Davidson believed God designed the Great Pyramid, he saw the factor as showing the extent to which Man is 'displaced' from perfection (God). In this sense, the Displacement Factor is the exact value of Man's will.

However, we believe the builders carried out God's intentions precisely. He could only have drawn up His schedule after having calculated the mathematical value of Man's free will, therefore this value had to be incorporated in the Great Pyramid. We are the first to realise this, and the reason why He did so.

Once God had arrived at a mathematical value for free will – human potential – He could divide mankind into groups of varying strengths and line them up like pawns and pieces at the start of a game of chess.

In a game of chess, the player who moves first uses pieces coloured white and his opponent replies with pieces coloured black. The colours symbolise good and evil. We may assume that God handles the white pieces, but He needs an evil opponent to handle the black pieces, and He has an opponent who exactly matches this description: the Devil.

We have thus provided a logical basis for the oldest figurative expression of chess: a duel between God and the Devil, with the future of mankind at stake.

Therefore the dates/events in the time-line are the key moves in a game of living chess between God and the Devil.

Neither God nor the Devil can override our free will, but God has an advantage inasmuch as we can turn to Him for advice through prayer. However, thanks to free will we will come to know both good and evil.

* * * * * * *

There are many different ways of opening a game of chess, but we may assume God selected an opening that met His overriding priority: to move His Chosen Race to their place of destiny. This explains why Abraham went to Canaan, and Jacob led the Israelites to Egypt for God to inculcate them with His wisdom. However, the necessity for God to arrange the Exodus shows the actions of the Egyptians in a new light, as they enabled the Devil to prevent God from carrying out the final stage of His opening plan.

Every move in the game impacted on people, therefore God must have been able to communicate His moves to those affected. The only facility that offers such a means of communication is the two-way internet facility in our souls that God created so we could pray to Him and He could offer advice, hence God ordered the Israelites to pray to Him regularly and frequently. The fact that both Abraham and Jacob moved in the way God intended after receiving His advice shows that they did indeed use this facility.

The impact made by each move generates thoughts that create a file, and this is ultimately archived to our souls. We may assume God carefully analysed the consequences of each move before playing it, consequently He archives His analysis in the same file as the moves, to provide us with guidance for the future. But since His analysis includes moves that He believes the Devil will make, incorporating His analysis in our souls also embeds the Devil. We thus come to know through prayer God's concept of evil (the Devil's thinking) as well as coming to know evil through the exercise of our free will.

The fact that the Devil is incorporated into our thinking through data supplied by God explains why people carry out the Devil's work – upset God's plans – even though they think they are obeying God's commands. Religions that worship God in different ways have fought each other to the death because they believed God wished to be worshipped in only one way, yet the death of each adherent only furthered the Devil's plans.

Clearly God's analysis included the possibility of religious wars, and zealots believe they have to follow His analysis to the letter, whatever the consequences. The fact that these wars have the same relentlessness and ruthlessness that characterises the duel between God and Devil is clear proof that the Devil enters the thoughts of the combatants by proxy.

* * * * * * *

In our souls we possess a complete record of the game, together with God's analysis, and this means we can access both not only by prayer but also by hypnotic regression. God and the Devil had to plan far in advance, therefore God's analysis represents moves that are ahead of history. Consequently anyone able to access His analysis sees events still to come. We believe the analysis can be accessed not only by prayer and hypnotic regression but also by self-hypnosis, for this would explain why prophets and seers go into a dream-like state or trance before delivering their prophecies.

We have thus provided a logical basis for the accuracy of Old Testament prophecies.

In 487 B.C. Zechariah (9.9) predicted that Jesus would enter Jerusalem on an ass, and the populace would greet him as the promised Messiah. Their cries of "Hosanna" and strewing of palm branches, available only in the autumn, give his date of entry as Tabernacles, again as predicted by Zechariah (14.16).

In 758 B.C. Isaiah (7.14) predicted "a virgin shall conceive and bear a son, and shall call his name Immanuel [God with us]." The Virgin Mary duly gave birth to Jesus, who was described by the angel Gabriel as "of the Holy Ghost," meaning God-like. In 712 B.C. Isaiah (53.8-9) predicted, "He was taken from prison for judgement...and made his grave with the wicked and the rich. He had done no violence nor been deceitful." Jesus was indeed taken from prison and arraigned with other criminals before Pontius Pilate, the Roman governor. Jesus said nothing in answer to the charges put before him, and after his death certain of his followers took him down from the cross and laid him in the tomb of a rich merchant.

The prophets prepared people for Jesus' arrival. The necessity to pave the way for him becomes clear when we consider the old saying, "if a god suddenly appeared, people would either worship him or kill him," the reason being that a god would threaten to change everything, powerful interests in the old order would lose everything, and therefore would conspire to kill him.

That Jesus was well aware of this danger is evident from the fact that he said, "Think not that I am come to send peace on earth: I came not to send peace, but a sword. For I am come to set a son against his father, the daughter against her mother, and the daughter-in-law against her mother-in-law. And a man's foes shall be they of his own household" (Matthew 10.34-36). Then Jesus entrusted to Peter (his 'Rock') the task of establishing a church that would live on after his ministry,[21] and began to talk of his crucifixion.

One of Jesus' first acts was to declare himself The King of Israel, an announcement that was bound to infuriate powerful interests such as the Jewish authorities, but God had foreseen this and given legitimacy to Jesus' claim. Jesus was born into the House of David, David was the first anointed king of Israel, and could trace his ancestry back to Abraham. Jesus thus had royal lineage and, being immortal, fulfilled a promise God had made to David in 1042 B.C. with the words, "I will establish the throne of [your] kingdom forever."

Jesus was the fulfilment of the prophets and the history of the Israelites dating back to Abraham. This is God's strategy on the grand scale, flawless analysis of two thousand years!

* * * * * * *

The analysis extended even further. Jesus chose disciples who were totally unqualified for the tasks he had in store for them, yet they succeeded admirably. Simon and his brother, Andrew, were fishermen; the same applies to James, the son of Zebedee, and John, his brother. More surprising still, Jesus enlisted a tax-gatherer (Matthew), a profession as unpopular then as it is now.

Since the disciples fulfilled Jesus' expectations by spreading Christianity throughout the known world, Christians believe Jesus must have been guided in his selection by divine understanding of the qualities in men's souls. However, we showed that our souls are

21 Simon received a new name meaning 'Rock' after saying to Jesus, "Thou art the Christ, the Son of the living God." Jesus replied, "flesh and blood hath not revealed it to thee, but my Father which is in heaven" (Matthew 16.16-17). This can only mean God had incorporated Peter's rôle as the Church into His schedule.

protected by an encryption or format that neither God nor the Devil can breach, so the same must apply to Jesus. Besides, it would not explain how Jesus knew that he had to go to Galilee, because this required analysis of the future.

Likewise it also required analysis of the future for Jesus to be certain that he had done enough to ensure the spread of Christianity, because anyone else living at the time – or in the three centuries following his crucifixion – would have been far from certain that success was assured.

This is because Jesus wrote no book, did not give his teachings in systematic form, and did not found an organisation for perpetuating his religion. He entrusted to Peter (his 'Rock') the task of establishing a church, but Peter suffered martyrdom in Rome. Furthermore Peter, like the other leading Apostles, stressed the similarities between the teachings of Jesus and Judaism, which meant Christianity was in danger of being subsumed into Judaism.

Paul was chiefly responsible for preventing this outcome, but he did not convert to Christianity until after Jesus had been crucified. Moreover, prior to his conversion, Paul had been an ardent opponent of the faith, contributing to the persecution of believers. Indeed, he was on his way to Damascus to arrest Christians when Jesus appeared to him in a vision. Therefore Paul was not a natural choice for the task of preserving and spreading Christianity, yet he succeeded to such an extent that there can be no doubt Jesus made the right choice. Given that Jesus could not have read Paul's mind in order to gauge his character and abilities, the only explanation for his intercepting Paul is that God foresaw Paul making this journey and knew Jesus would succeed in converting him.

But even after Paul had been converted, the New Testament shows that he only preserved Christianity as a distinct faith through prodigious exertions. Furthermore, he came in for severe criticism from the leading apostles, who had remained in Jerusalem. Consequently Paul's success was by no means guaranteed, hence God must have known beforehand that he would succeed, and Jesus could enter Jerusalem, where God knew he would be crucified.

God must have determined the dates of Jesus' crucifixion and resurrection long beforehand, in order to draw up His schedule,[22] therefore it could be argued that Jesus' mission was cut short due to his betrayal by Judas Iscariot, and but for this he would have overrun God's schedule. However, it was not a random factor, because Jesus (and therefore God) knew Judas would betray him and it would not upset God's schedule. At the Last Supper, Jesus said to his disciples, "But behold, the hand of him that betrayeth me is with me at this table. And truly the Son of God goeth, as it was determined" (Luke 22.21-22).

The last line is the most telling, for it can only mean Judas' betrayal fitted in perfectly with God's schedule.

* * * * * * *

It is clear that the Bible is nothing less than the record of the moves in a game of chess between God and the Devil, together with God's analysis of His strategy and tactics, some of which stretch far into the future. Its sixty-six books read like the unfolding of a strategy, and therefore can be regarded as one book. Each book is complete in itself, with its own theme and analysis, just like the individual moves in a game of chess.

Originally God's strategy was for the Israelites to receive His wisdom and deliver it to the rest of the world, but He had to come up with another idea after the Israelites failed to gain access to the Great Pyramid. The new strategy was for Jesus to preach His words (the

---

22 Jesus knew at the outset how his life would end, because even before entrusting his Church to Peter he had spoken of his death and resurrection, e.g., "For as Jonas was three days and three nights in the whale's belly, so shall the Son of man be three days and three nights in the heart of the earth" (Matthew 12.40).

Gospel), his apostles to deliver it to the rest of the world, and to explain it in the Epistles.

Strategy entails tactics. We have already illustrated some of these in the previous section, but each book of the Bible can be regarded as a tactic, and they flow logically: the books of Old Testament prepare the way for Jesus; the Gospels present him to the world; in the Acts he is preached and his Gospel is delivered to the world; in the Epistles his Gospel is explained; and Revelation is God's analysis of the future.

The fact that God had to revise His strategy, yet there is no trace of this in the grouping, shows that He seamlessly incorporated His original plan into the revised version.

Thus coverage of the central theme – the mission of the Israelites – shows no inconsistencies despite spanning the Old and New Testaments: to testify on behalf of God in the midst of universal idolatry (Deuteronomy 6.4; Isaiah 43.10); to illustrate to other nations the greater blessings from serving the one true God (Deuteronomy 33.26-29, 1 Chronicles 17.20-21, Psalms 102.15); to receive and preserve the divine revelation (Romans 3.1-2); and to produce Jesus, Man's Saviour and Lord (Romans 9.4).

In a similarly orderly manner the Bible sets out the arrival of Jesus, his Person as "God manifest in the flesh" (1 Timothy 3.16), his transfiguration, sacrificial death, resurrection, and ascension (the Gospels).

After Jesus ascends, the remaining books follow logically: the Gospel is preached in the Acts and explained in the Epistles; in Revelation God predicts the success of His strategy.

The Bible was compiled by some forty-four writers over a period of twenty centuries, and the fact that they, without collusion, produced a work of perfect harmony that progressively unfolds, means they must have been accessing one source. Given the nature of the material, the only possible source was God's analysis. This is unanswerable proof that the Bible was divinely inspired.

Part 4

Games of chess develop in accordance with the nature of the opening. In the opening God developed His Chosen Race, consequently subsequent dates in His schedule must relate to it. Since these dates are also relevant to British history, both races must be crucial to the success of God's plan and His schedule.

Our conclusion strengthens the theory that there is a special relationship between the British and Israelis – Anglo-Israelism. The roots of the theory lie not only in the Great Pyramid[23] but also in the Bible.

The link with the Bible arises from the prophecy of Daniel. When Daniel was taken out of Jerusalem and enslaved by Nebuchadnezzar, the year was 603 B.C. By interpreting a dream, he prophesied this was the beginning of a long time in exile for the Jews from their capital city. According to Anglo-Israelists, he said the gentiles would hold Jerusalem for seven cycles. Each cycle was a period of 360 years, corresponding to one degree of a circle. Then, at the beginning of the seventh cycle, the great 'stone race' would rise up and rule the world. At the end of the seventh cycle, this same race would release Jerusalem from the gentiles and give it back to the Jews. Starting from 603 B.C., the seventh cycle began in December-January 1557-8, which is when Elizabeth I became Queen and England became a superpower. Exactly 360 years later, in December 1917, General Allenby marched a British army into Jerusalem and rid it of the Turks. Subsequently the British government returned Jerusalem to the Jews, as had been prophesied.

* * * * * * *

23 There is undoubtedly a link between the British inch and the pyramid inch, for the people who designed Stonehenge used the latter. The inner circle of this megalith has a precise diameter of 3,652.42 pyramid inches, so the entire circular area would fit precisely into one quarter of the base of the Great Pyramid. This suggests early inhabitants of the British Isles were related to the 'lost tribes' of Israel.

Given Britain's rôle in God's plan, attempts to bring about her destruction or conquest must originate from the Devil, and this gives an entirely new meaning to Philip II's attempt in 1588 to conquer Elizabethan England by means of the Spanish Armada, and Napoleon's later attempts. We also have to view Elizabethan heroes such as Sir Francis Drake, Grenville and Hawkins, plus John Churchill, who defeated the army of Louis XIV at the Battle of Blenheim in 1704, together with Nelson and the Duke of Wellington, not as fortuitous appearances but as divine interventions.

The same context applies to events in the twentieth century that threatened Britain's survival, especially as it was only by an extraordinary convergence of several isolated factors that she was forced into the First World War.

The most notable factor was the sudden emergence of Germany as a national power after nearly two thousand years of multiple fractures. Its industrial output grew apace and by 1900 exceeded that of Great Britain. At the same time the population grew rapidly, and to meet its ever-increasing demands Germany expanded overseas, hoping to establish an empire that would rival the British. It also developed a powerful navy, and by 1913 the German army was widely believed to be the most powerful in the world.

These developments produced a wave of national pride, and to show that it stood at the forefront of nations, Germany tore up treaties with France and Russia, aligning itself instead with the Austro-Hungarian and Ottoman empires. This forced France and Great Britain to become allies, thus creating a balance of power, but meanwhile the political map of the Balkans became so peculiarly drawn that it brought all these powers into direct conflict.

The Balkans consisted of various kingdoms peopled by Serbs, Croats and Slovenes. These were part of the Austrian Hapsburg Empire, but they fitted uneasily, because the Serbs and Slovenes had a natural affinity with the Russians. Austria was supported by Germany, hence

France and Great Britain allied themselves with Russia to produce a theoretical balance of power.

This mirrors so closely the rivalry between God and the Devil that one is not surprised that it was brought about by extraordinary developments. One can also believe that the Devil supported Austria and Germany, because God would have backed the British, in confirmation of the rôle delineated for them in the prophecy of Daniel.

The descent to war began in 1914, when a Serb assassinated the Austrian Archduke Franz Ferdinand. Both Austria and Germany sought to punish Serbia, which immediately turned to Russia for help. Shots were exchanged between Germany and Russia on 1st August 1914, which immediately brought France and Great Britain into the war.

For three years there was trench warfare and virtual stalemate, until the USA entered the war and Germany swiftly capitulated. During these years, there was slaughter on an unprecedented scale – millions of soldiers died on both sides, and the talents of generations were lost.

One can now see why the Devil waited until the twentieth century to destroy the British. The prophecy of Daniel was close to fulfilment, Man had fashioned weapons of war that were far more destructive than in previous ages, and he was ruthless enough to make full use of them. Even when an Armistice was declared, the six hours that elapsed before hostilities officially ceased saw heavy fighting and thousands of unnecessary casualties.

* * * * * * *

The surrender of Germany thwarted the Devil's desire to destroy Britain, but he had another weapon at his disposal. The war had wrecked Britain's economy, and the loss of so many young men during the fighting meant that recovery, if at all possible, would be slow and painful. Therefore the decline of commodity prices on the London Stock Exchange fitted perfectly into his plans. It began on 29th May

1928, the same date as the starting-point for the 'Veil of Tribulation and Humility' in the time-line.

The collapse affected the USA, but this has to be viewed in the same context as Britain's economic woes. The USA had come to Britain's rescue in the war, so now the USA came within the Devil's sphere of operations.

In one month, starting 23rd October 1929, prices on Wall Street – the New York Stock Exchange – fell $26 billion. Millions of people lost their savings, over 3,000 banks closed, many more companies were forced out of business, and unemployment soared.

The economic deterioration in the USA had a serious affect on Europe, which relied on USA markets and capital. As USA overseas investments evaporated, Germany and Austria approached bankruptcy. With the loss of its USA customers, Britain was forced off the gold standard. International trade and payments, which had operated freely, were soon restricted by import quotas, tariff walls, restrictions on the exchange of gold and currencies, and various other nationalistic devices intended to protect one economy at the expense of others. As farmers throughout the world vainly sought markets for their high output, commodity prices fell to fractions of their 1929 values.

Protectionist policies amongst European nations led to the rise of nationalist movements, notably Fascism in Italy and Spain, and Nazism in Germany. The leaders of these movements eventually seized control and dominated the 1930s. Their names are amongst the most infamous in history: Franco (Spain), Mussolini (Italy) and, worst of all, Hitler (Germany). The last two-named would soon go to war against Britain, hence all the above developments were stages in the Devil's strategy: destroy the economies of Britain and the USA at the same time as confronting them with formidable military opponents.

Part 5

The critical stage was reached on 16th September 1936. According to the Great Pyramid's time-line, the date marks the end of the 'Veil of Tribulation and Humility' and the entrance to the Hall of Judgement. Pyramidologists interpret this to mean it heralds the Age of Aquarius, and this would explain why an uncharacteristic wave of pacifism came over the British. However, the wave occurred at exactly the same time as Mussolini and Hitler succeeded in converting Italy and Germany respectively into military superpowers, so one would imagine that war was inevitable, especially as the Devil had contrived to ensure that Britain was far less well-prepared than it had been for the First World War.

Yet the time-line in the Great Pyramid makes no mention of the Second World War!

This is an extraordinary omission, given the accuracy of the time-line so far and the fact that the Second World War was a greater threat to Britain's survival than had been the clearly delineated First World War.

The only explanation for the omission is that the Second World War did not occur in the game between God and the Devil. However, this means the 20th August 1953 was Judgement Day for someone else!

Who could it be? It had to be someone exactly like us, and there is only one candidate: Man's forerunners!

They had lived on a world that corresponded to Earth, and God had endowed them with free will, hence He only had to analyse their behaviour to arrive at the mathematical value of our free will.

* * * * * * *

God and the Devil played a game of living chess before the beginning of Time to see how the future of our forerunners would unfold, and this is the game whose key moves are recorded in the time-line.

God must have arrived at the value of free will by analysing our forerunners' behaviour after they had been banished from the Garden of Eden, and incorporating this value into our personalities. To ensure that we would repeat our forerunners' history, He decided the order in which Man appeared, and then tried to control the number and quality of mankind. This explains the order in which Adam and Eve (Man) made their entrances into the Garden of Eden, and the strictures that God imposed on them.

After Adam and Eve (Man) were banished from the Garden, God could still decide which souls would be despatched to Earth because He has continuous access to souls whilst they reside in Heaven. This provides Him with a direct means of controlling Man's qualities at any given point in history.

The advantage this accrues to God is fully in accordance with the logic of chess, because it equals the slight advantage that the player of the white pieces always enjoys at the outset of the game. White makes the opening move, and this gives him the initiative because he can make the running by dictating the nature of the opening. Eventually, however, the player of the black pieces will equalise by bringing all his pieces into play. By analogy the Devil (black) will eventually equalise because Man will come to know evil.

However, at some point and for some unknown reason we diverged from the original game between God and the Devil. We have to discover when and why we did so.

* * * * * * *

Man's forerunners would not have experienced the Age of Aquarius because it was created by the movements of stars in our universe, therefore they would not have experienced the wave of pacifism that engulfed many people in the 1930s. This is a critical factor because the divergence must have occurred in the mid-1930s. The time-line correctly predicted that commodity prices would begin to decline on the London stock market on 29th May 1928, and global economic and financial systems would collapse in the following decade – the 'Veil of Tribulation and Humility'.

The collapse propelled Hitler and his Nazi Party to power. In 1933 he became Chancellor of Germany and, after the death of Hindenburg the following year, took the title of Führer ('leader'). War broke out on 1st September 1939, but it had been inevitable at least a year earlier, when Britain and France failed at Munich in 1938 to punish Hitler for his illegal annexation of Austria, and Hitler, a month before the outbreak of war, had neutralised the USSR by signing a non-aggression pact.

Therefore the divergence occurred after Hitler became Führer but before the Munich Agreement of 1938.

This means God would have been aware of Hitler's propensity for evil and the imminence of war but, not being handicapped by the pacifism induced in the British by the onset of the Age of Aquarius and which had persuaded them to elect Neville Chamberlain as Prime Minister, He had the time and the means to avert the Second World War – by using the promotion rule in chess[24] to promote Winston Churchill as UK Prime Minister.

Churchill viewed Nazism as an evil that had to be destroyed, and he had an unwavering fighting spirit. He urged Chamberlain to increase Britain's military might, but Chamberlain refused. He knew Germany was stronger than Britain from a military standpoint, and was afraid to provoke it, hence his policy of appeasement. But Churchill was undaunted. He believed God was on his side, because Nazism threatened to destroy the civilised world, and therefore the forces of right would prevail, despite the odds against them.

If Churchill had been Prime Minister, then we believe Hitler would have backed down. He would not have gone to war, because he would have seen in Churchill an implacable opponent who would use every

24 In chess, pawns – the weakest units – that reach the opponent's back rank can be promoted to the most powerful piece on the board.

means at his disposal to destroy him. Moreover, Hitler did not want to fight the British, because he believed there was a natural empathy between the Aryan and Anglo-Saxon races.

Without the Second World War, however, Hitler would have remained in power, and the consequences for mankind would have been disastrous.

Hitler was driven by an ideology that divided humanity into Aryans and subhumans. He was obsessed with *Lebensraum*, or "living space" for Germany, which he pursued through a policy of ruthless expansion. His scientists conducted research into nuclear weapons, and in 1939 four scientists working in Berlin – Otto Hahn, Lise Meitner, F. Strassmann, and Otto Frisch – found the key. They discovered that a neutron, when introduced into a uranium nucleus by a radioactive bombardment, split the nucleus in two, releasing more neutrons and tremendous energy. This suggested the fission of uranium could start a chain reaction.

This discovery should have given Hitler a tremendous advantage, but he had created a political atmosphere in Germany that caused a mass exodus of nuclear scientists to the USA. Unfortunately the USA government showed little interest, because research into nuclear capability was hugely expensive and the country was in the grip of economic depression.

In 1939 German scientists grasped the implications of fission discovery and launched an intensive investigation. Later that year President Roosevelt, on the advice of a committee set up to consider the feasibility of constructing a nuclear bomb, recommended further research be supported by government funds.

To produce the chain reaction required for a nuclear explosion, fissionable material in the bomb must exceed a certain size ('critical mass'). American scientists knew this mass was 100 kilograms (less for uranium), but German scientists thought it was far greater, and told Hitler that a nuclear bomb was unfeasible. However, the US government only began to accelerate the nuclear weapons programme after it entered the Second World War, when it changed the emphasis from research to implementation. Without this impetus, research would have continued at a more leisurely pace, giving German scientists sufficient time to correct their mistake and place nuclear weapons at Hitler's disposal.

Russian scientists were also seeking to create nuclear weapons and had gone one stage further, realising that nuclear fusion was a superior source of explosive energy. It dispenses with the need for critical mass, and so a fusion bomb can theoretically be made as large as desired. This type of bomb is known as a hydrogen bomb (H-bomb) or thermonuclear device.

Scientists in the USA also understood the advantages of the H-bomb, but the government gave little support, and no actual development or testing was done until 1950. This was in response to the detonation by the USSR of its first fission-type weapon in 1949, which signified the end of the USA's nuclear weapons monopoly. More than that, it indicated the USSR would probably soon have the ability to make an H-bomb. Further indications of the USSR's potential came with the confession of Klaus Fuchs, a scientist who had participated in important research on nuclear and thermonuclear weapons, that he had transmitted classified information to the USSR.

At last the US government woke up, and President Truman, on 13th January 1951, ordered accelerated development of the H-bomb. A massive thermonuclear device was detonated in November 1952, producing the first true thermonuclear explosion, with a yield estimated at several megatons (millions of tons) of TNT. On 20th August 1953, the Russians detonated their first H-bomb.

This created a balance between the two superpowers, but they had reached this result by luck and the military priorities of the Second World War. Without the war we reach two completely different scenarios by 20th August 1953. The USA and the UK, having conducted research into nuclear weaponry at a leisurely pace, are far behind Germany and Russia, which have been engaged in a furious arms race. Alternatively, all the major powers, including Germany and Britain (British scientists were not far behind the Americans), possess nuclear and thermonuclear weapons.

In both cases Hitler would have been able to deploy nuclear weapons by the date specified in the Great Pyramid. Since his rabid view of mankind would not have allowed him to tolerate a situation where the Russians had any degree of superiority, he would undoubtedly have heeded the Devil as he told him how to exploit an object that contained the nuclear power of every atom.

We may never know how Hitler's scientists succeeded in unleashing this power, but we do know when they did, because the time-line in the Great Pyramid ends abruptly at midnight 22nd September 2001. This must have been the date of the Big Bang.

* * * * * * *

Our analysis leads to some extraordinary conclusions. Firstly, God's tactic of promoting Churchill to the UK premiership meant our forerunners avoided the Second World War but had no way of avoiding nuclear war and the Big Bang!

Since we experienced the Second World War but not the Big Bang, the Second World War must have been Man's salvation!

The war led directly to Hitler's demise, therefore Neville Chamberlain, though universally reviled today for his policy of appeasement towards Hitler, actually played a vital part in securing Man's salvation! His policy induced Hitler to launch the attack against Poland that led to the Second World War, and Chamberlain remained Prime Minister long enough to prevent Churchill from succeeding to this post until after the war had begun!

Part 6

One might think that we owe our salvation to luck rather than calculation, yet there are good reasons for believing God was in control of events all along.

For Man, the significance of 20th August 1953 was that it began the Age of Aquarius – a period of harmony and understanding – but it had a lengthy transitional period, and the evidence shows that Man began to come under its influence in the mid-1930s.

A wave of pacifism swept across Britain and elsewhere. Such thinking was much more in keeping with Chamberlain's policies than those of Churchill, which explains why the former became Prime Minister. This showed the power of the new age and, since it would increase with each passing day, Hitler could not afford to ignore it. He had to acquire and deploy nuclear weapons before its onset.

Hitler would have been well aware of the closing date, because he had a profound belief in astrology. On one occasion his life had been saved by the prediction of an astrologer. In 1939, a Swiss mathematician named Krafft wrote a letter to a member of Himmler's Intelligence Service predicting that Hitler's life would be in danger from "explosives" between the 7th and 10th November. In fact, Hitler missed death from a bomb by only a few minutes on 8th November 1939. Krafft was brought to Berlin, and for a time became a semi-official astrologer to the Nazis.

Once we view the period from the outbreak of the Second World War until the 20th August 1953 as one in which Hitler had to deploy nuclear weapons, then we can account for the two disastrous mistakes that brought about his defeat.

The first was to forego completing the defeat of Britain, whose forces had been driven out of Europe, and instead to invade the USSR, with whom he had signed a peace treaty. Hitler had to acquire nuclear weapons quickly, and he had to employ Russian scientists, because his own scientists had failed him. Therefore the conquest of Russia was his top priority. This explains why he ordered his armies to advance at full speed into Russia, despite the risk that they would over-stretch their supply lines.

The second was to persuade the Japanese, with whom he had entered a pact in 1940, to attack the USA, because this would embroil the USA in a war in the Pacific rather than in Europe, where it would speedily have brought about his defeat.

Both decisions rebounded on Hitler. The USA not only declared war against Japan but simultaneously declared war on Germany. Furthermore, it had sufficient military might both to defeat the Japanese and turn the tide of war in Europe. Hitler's decision to invade the USSR also rebounded, for his forces, like those of Napoleon a century earlier, became frozen in the Russian winter.

Our explanation for these decisions is the only one that fits the facts. The Japanese attack on the American fleet in Pearl Harbour on 7th December 1941, which signalled the start of their offensive, occurred at the same time as Hitler's forces were advancing on Moscow. Moreover, the Japanese constituted a threat to Russia's eastern provinces that Russia could not ignore, and in deploying troops to protect these regions, Russia had to reduce the number of troops that confronted Hitler's armies.

In addition, there was no necessity for Hitler to abandon his plan to invade Britain. The RAF was almost exhausted, and could not have contested air supremacy for much longer. Once the *Luftwaffe* had gained control of the skies, Hitler could have launched his planned invasion of Britain and, after its conquest, concentrated more forces against Russia.

Therefore from a strictly military viewpoint, Hitler could have won the war by consolidating his hold on Europe, defeating Britain, and then invading Russia. Nor should we doubt that Hitler had sufficient understanding of military strategy to appreciate this. His decision to invade Poland and push for total war flew in the face of advice from army leaders that Germany had insufficient strength to defeat the Allied powers, but successive conquests of Denmark, Norway, Luxembourg, Holland, Belgium, and finally France vindicated Hitler's judgement.

Consequently by allowing Britain to remain as a potential threat on his western flank whilst deploying his armies east to Russia, Hitler committed an uncharacteristic error, and this can only be explained by the need to meet a schedule that was so tight it gave him insufficient time to adopt the safe military course.

Therefore the course of the Second World War can only be understood in the context of God's schedule, which imposed on Hitler the necessity to acquire and employ nuclear weapons before the 20th August 1953. Without this closing date, the war would have taken a very different course, and could have been disastrous for the whole of mankind.

In this respect, Hitler was fated to lose, so his defeat can be ascribed to God's foresight in arranging for the movement of stars to reach the Age of Aquarius before Hitler had time to defeat Britain and conquer Russia. This means God was in control from start to finish.[25]

---

25 Our analysis of the Second World War and its aftermath strengthens a strand of the Anglo-Israelism theory that is linked to Hebrew history. It is believed by those who profess the theory that the Anglo-Saxon race is the surviving representative of the 'Ten Lost Tribes' who were supposed to have migrated westward and settled in Ireland, becoming the ancestors of the British and American peoples. The tribe would be put in charge of the world during the time of 'Judgement', which the time-line in the Great Pyramid shows as starting on the 16th September 1936.
The same date is given in Revelation as the "sounding of the Seventh Trumpet", and marks the beginning of the "times of the end". The end comes with Armageddon. This, we believe, must refer to the end of the game of chess between God and Devil, in which Russia detonated its first H-bomb on 20th August 1953 and triggered a full-scale nuclear war.
We avoided this fate, but the seventeen-year period still has great significance for us, because the 20th August 1953 is the date on which we entered the Age of Aquarius and had to end our previous attitude towards war. In this sense it became a time of 'Judgement' on earlier conflicts.
During these seventeen years the USA and Great Britain, with its vast Empire,

Part 7

For God to produce an improvement at such a late stage in Man's history would come as no surprise to chess grandmasters. Their games are recorded, and everyone studies them to find improvements that they can spring on unsuspecting opponents. We may assume God recorded the moves of His game with the Devil, studied them in detail, discovered where He had gone wrong, and devised an improvement.

When God recreated Man and endowed him with free will, He was actually releasing the Devil from imprisonment in the Pit so that they could play an after-game – a sequel to the history of our forerunners – and in this game, despite all the Devil's machinations, God's prepared improvement would be bound to appear.

Since God's improvement relied on Earth entering the Age of Aquarius at a precise moment in time, we can now understand why He chose the Milky Way to be our galaxy, situated the Solar System at a precise distance from, and in a precise orbit around, the centre of our galaxy, situated Earth in a particular orbit around the Sun and in a region of the Solar System where the other planets would cause it to precess, and, to meet this last requirement, made fine adjustments to Earth's size and angle of tilt.

All these factors are incorporated into the exterior of the Great Pyramid, which is irrefutable proof that the builders were working directly from God's blueprint!

The 'pyramidal inch' – 1.0011 inches – is the basic unit of measurement in the structure. It is based on the actual size of the Earth, because it is precisely one five-hundred millionth the distance from

---

were the major powers and effectively reigned supreme. They 'passed judgement' on Hitler and his evil Nazi Party, as well as on their counterparts in Italy – Mussolini and his Fascist Party – by destroying them in the Second World War. They also had military supremacy over Russia and its communist allies until 1953. The parallel with the Anglo-Israelism theory and the chronology in the Great Pyramid could hardly be closer.

the North Pole to the South Pole. This required the designer to have calculated exactly Earth's polar diameter, but no designer 6,000 years ago had this ability, so God must have supplied the information.

Using the pyramidal inch, an amazing series of measurements unfold. The circumference of the Great Pyramid is 36,524.22 pyramid inches, which is the number of days in a solar year multiplied by 100, or the number of days in a century.

To remove any suspicion that this measurement was coincidental, the Great Pyramid embodies the other three "years" of Earth's orbit by means of a hollowing-in of its faces. The base length of each side is 9,131.05 pyramid inches, or 365.242 sacred cubits, the number of days in a year. From the base of the hollow to the edge of the face in both directions gives a value of 365.256 sacred cubits, which is the sideral year (the time taken by Earth to orbit the Sun in relation to a fixed star). The difference of about twenty minutes *per annum*, caused by precession is also incorporated in the Great Pyramid's structure (see below). The deepest point of penetration at the hollow to the edges of the faces gives a value of 365.259 sacred cubits, which is precisely the number of days in the anomalistic year. This is the amount of time it takes Earth to travel from perihelion, the closest point to the Sun, back to perihelion.

The height of the Great Pyramid multiplied by ten million gives the approximate distance between Earth and the Sun. One pyramidal inch multiplied by 100 million gives the average distance covered by the Earth in its orbit around the Sun – it could not be more exact because the elliptical nature of Earth's orbit gives a mean variation of 3 million miles.

Earth's polar axis inclines to a different point in space each day, and does not attain its original position for almost 26,000 years. This phenomenon is known as precession. It causes the equinoxes to move westward along the ecliptic – the path of Aquarius – at the rate of 1° in 72 years, and this is monumentalised in the Great Pyramid. The sum of the base diagonals is 25,826.5 pyramid inches, which is exactly the number of years in the total circuit of precession. Moreover, the perimeter measurement of the Great Pyramid at the thirty-fifth course of masonry, which is a course of greater width than the others, also equals the precessional circuit of 25,826.5 years.

These are the key calculations God had to make to ensure that Earth entered the Age of Aquarius exactly on schedule, and to emphasise the fact that everything in the Great Pyramid is mathematically perfect, God designed it to monumentalise the circle and give the correct value of pi. The value is 3.14159, a figure obtained by dividing the sum distance of its side by twice its height – the usual method of calculating the relation of a circumference to its radius.[26]

The Great Pyramid is God's way of saying He did everything He could to ensure that we avoided the fate of our forerunners.

The Great Pyramid is God's monument to Man.

* * * * * * *

Given that God was addressing all mankind, one might have expected Him to inscribe His message on other ancient monuments, particularly the pyramids in Central and South America, but the data is unique to the Great Pyramid. It was therefore purpose-built, and we can prove this to be the case because there are extraordinary facts concerning its orientation and location.

The Great Pyramid is orientated to the cardinal points of the compass. This meant the designer had determined and located true north, a feat that would have been beyond the understanding of anyone living at the time of its construction. Renaissance astronomer Tycho Brahe set out to orient his observatory at Urambourg to true north, but missed by eight minutes of arc; today we have gyroscopes and orbiting

26 Archimedes never got closer than 3.14128, and he made his calculations thousands of years after the Great Pyramid had been built!

satellites to determine north, yet without any of these aids the Great Pyramid was perfectly oriented.[27]

Not only was the Great Pyramid perfectly orientated, but it was also situated at the junction of the prime meridian and the Tropic of Capricorn. The prime meridian is a line from the north to south poles, and it crosses the greatest mass of land on Earth's north-south axis. Likewise the line going around the globe from west to east on the Great Pyramid's precise latitude also passes through more land mass than any other. This means that the Great Pyramid was situated at the centre of Earth's land mass and exactly quarters that mass – clearly the only possible location for a monument containing God's message to all mankind!

27 The Great Pyramid is slightly twisted to the left, missing true north by about four minutes of arc, but the Second and Third Pyramids on the Giza plateau are also slightly twisted, suggesting that earthquakes or subsidence have affected their orientation. Two other explanations were put forward in the March 1973 issue of *Science* magazine by two researchers who, after stating that the Great Pyramid was perfectly orientated, said that its slight misalignment was due either to a shift of Earth's pole or movement of the African continent. It was definitely not the fault of the builders!

MAN'S PROGRESS, FUTURE AND DESTINY

Chapter One

Man's Progess

Part 1

In the mid-1930s we diverged from the history of our forerunners, and the only prediction God could make was that we would enter the Age of Aquarius on 20th August 1953. We entered on schedule, but meanwhile governments and the United Nations (UN) had taken decisions that meant our future would take a completely different course from that of our forerunners.

We thus entered uncharted waters, and this explains why no more events are recorded in the time-line in the Great Pyramid.

However, one fact never changes, and that is the never-ending duel between God and the Devil. This duel is replicated on Earth, because God incorporated good and evil into our personalities. It is the context in which to view human history.

God and the Devil are closely-matched, hence the same applies to good and evil on Earth.

The clearest illustration of how the personal nature of the duel is mirrored in events on Earth is the Second World War, because the leading combatants, Winston Churchill and Adolf Hitler, personified good and evil respectively.

Hitler personified the evil at the heart of Nazism, Churchill believed

God was on his side because Nazism was a threat to the civilised world. Hitler had charisma and a personal magnetism that electrified audiences and galvanised Germany. Churchill had an extraordinary rapport with ordinary people, and united Britain to a far greater extent than any leader before or since.

This is the clearest illustration of the fact that Man's free will combines the qualities of God and the Devil. This in turn explains why the course of human history has been a ceaseless struggle between good and evil.

The closeness of this struggle is mirrored in the closeness of the struggle in the Second World War. At first Hitler had superior military forces ranged behind him, but Churchill believed the forces of right would ultimately prevail, despite the odds against them, and he was correct.

To prove our point that the duels are mirror-images, the confrontation between Churchill and Hitler could not have been coincidental because many unlikely factors had to converge.

Hitler's doctrine of Aryan supremacy and the necessity to exterminate various races, especially the Jews, should have been anathema to a civilised race such as the Germans, but it struck a chord owing the economic hardships they had suffered since the First World War.

Hitler founded the Nazi Party, but it was a minor political force until 1933, when it was suddenly propelled into government and Hitler was appointed to the most important office, Chancellor of Germany.

Churchill likewise languished in the political wilderness, but after the outbreak of war he was suddenly propelled to the British premiership.

Therefore both Churchill and Hitler rose simultaneously to power and pre-eminence by the most unlikely routes.

Part 2

The struggle between good and evil did not end with the Second World War. It continued afterwards, when Europe was divided between two superpowers with opposing ideologies. On one side were the USA and its allies. These nations were democratic and Christian. On the other side was the USSR, a communist country that rejected God. It also had allies – east European nations that it had conquered and forced to become communist.

At this stage the USA had a clear advantage, because it was the only nation capable of exploiting nuclear power. It had detonated three nuclear bombs over Japan to bring the war to an end, and now it intended to use nuclear power for peaceful purposes. However, espionage activity by Klaus Fuchs enabled the USA's nuclear secrets to be smuggled to the USSR, which proceeded to construct its own nuclear weapons.

The USSR was ruled by Stalin, whom many Russians regarded as more evil than Hitler. Indeed, if Hitler had made use of the 800,000 Russian troops who were prepared to fight Stalin, he would have defeated the USSR and won the war. Fortunately Hitler's racism, which regarded Russians as fit only for slavery, blinded him to this possibility.

Equally fortunately, God had prepared a back-up plan. At the very moment when the USSR detonated its first H-bomb, which could have triggered a nuclear war with the USA, Earth entered the Age of Aquarius - a period of peace and harmony.

We proved that God planned the conjunction, which shows that the preparations He made for our well-being extended far beyond our planet and the Solar System to encompass the movement of stars throughout the universe!

Part 3

The clearest illustration of the manner in which the duel between God and the Devil affects events on Earth today is the Arab-Israeli conflict in the Middle East.

The Arabs are determined to destroy Israel, which they view as an intrusion into Muslim territory, but Israel is supported by the West, which believes Israel has a right to exist. This means three religions – Christianity, Judaism and Islam – are locked in conflict, but this should not have led to bloodshed because there is literally common ground between them.

In Jerusalem, the Dome of the Rock covers one of the holiest spots in Islam. From this rock, legend says, the prophet Muhammad was transported one night to Heaven, where he met with God and received the teachings that constitute the Muslim religion. However, the same site is also of crucial importance to Jews and Christians. It is where Abraham offered to sacrifice his son Isaac, and it is the site of the Temple of Solomon.

Furthermore, Islam acknowledges the validity of Judaism and Christianity, but believes itself to be the fulfilment of them – to supersede and cancel them. Muslims believe Abraham, Moses and Jesus all preached Islam, but their teachings were changed by their followers into Judaism and Christianity, whereas Muhammad's preaching has been preserved unchanged, by the will of God.

Therefore another factor must be fuelling the fighting. This factor is God's duel with the Devil, for Israel is the homeland of the Jews – God's Chosen Race – consequently attacks on Israel are a threat to God's élite, His plan and His schedule.

Once we appreciate the paramount importance of Israel to God, then it comes as no surprise that Israel's principal supporters are leading Christian nations. This suggests that Muslims who attack Israel wish to undo God's plan, and are in league with the Devil, but this is unthinkable, because they accept certain tenets of Christianity and Judaism. Therefore Muslims must believe their attacks on Israel are in accordance with the wishes of God (Allah), but this means God is sending contradictory messages to Christians and Muslims!

The only way this contradiction could have arisen is if God had analysed the situation in the Middle East and incorporated into his analysis 'moves' that He believes the Devil will make to thwart His plans. The analysis would impact on the minds of the faithful, and lead to opposite reactions. Christians would adopt lines of analysis that accorded with their understanding of Jesus' teachings, and support the Israelis, but Muslims would not hesitate to attack them.

God had to analyse the situation in the Middle East because crucial decisions regarding its future were taken during the period when Man diverged from His schedule. Therefore God must have begun analysing after Man rejoined His schedule on 20th August 1953.

What God saw must have appalled Him: the State of Israel was hemmed in on three sides by implacably hostile Arab nations and had its back to the sea. Clearly Israel needed the support of the West, particularly the USA. However, this would pit Christians against Muslims – invoking memories of the Crusades – and pit the West's democratic principles – which Israel embraced – against nations ruled by Muslim clergy. Both would provide Muslims with reasons for wishing not only the destruction of Israel but also that of the West!

However, Israel receives sufficient support from the West to maintain a dominant military position. This was proved in dramatic fashion in 1967, when Israel pre-empted an invasion by its Arab neighbours – Egypt, Jordan and Syria – with military action that in six days not only extended its territory far beyond the limits laid down by the UN, but also secured vital military objectives. In the south, it occupied the Gaza Strip and the Sinai Desert, which completely neutralised Egypt as a potential threat. In the north, it took command of the Golan Heights, which enabled it to observe military operations in Syria and forestall another attack. But the most important prize was the West Bank of the river Jordan, for this included the city of Jerusalem.

Once again the biblical prophecy of Daniel had been fulfilled, and Jerusalem was under Jewish control. One is therefore tempted to conclude that this outcome was God's seal of approval on the establishment of the State of Israel, and that His analysis ended here.

But God must have looked further ahead, because the capture of Jerusalem by the Israelis was bound to increase the anger of Arabs, and indeed the entire region erupted into a full-scale war only six years later. Again Israel was victorious, and since then the Arab nations have avoided outright military confrontation.

However, hostilities have not ceased. Iran and Syria provide support for terrorist groups – militant Muslims or Islamists – who harass Israel unceasingly. One of these groups – Hamas – has recently seized control of South Palestine, from where it fires artillery shells and missiles into Israel.

The blows that each side rains down on the other have the same relentless quality as lines of analysis in which God has made His strongest moves and given the strongest replies of the Devil. This means the source of the unending enmity between Arabs and Jews is the unending enmity between God and the Devil plus the Devil's desire to destroy God's Chosen Race. It is therefore no coincidence that the fighting takes place around Armageddon, where the Bible predicts the Final Conflict between the armies of God and the Devil will be fought.

We can also add another factor: the Devil's desire for revenge after his hopes for an early end to Man's existence were dashed when God arranged for Earth to enter the Age of Aquarius at the very moment when the USA and USSR were on the brink of nuclear war. We believe this desire led to God and the Devil agreeing to play another game of chess for the future of mankind.

In this game the Devil would be entitled to make the first move, and he would naturally choose an opening that enabled him to launch an attack on God's forces. Assuming God had foreseen this threat, identified the main targets, and staged attacks in His pre-game analysis, we have the explanation for the sudden rise in the ferocity of Islamists, and their attacks on the West.

This suggests the Devil's first move was made on 11th September 2001, and resulted in the destruction by members of al-Qa'eda of the World Trade Centre in New York, with the loss of over 3,000 lives. God quickly replied, and the West, under the leadership of the USA, invaded Afghanistan, where al-Qa'eda and its leader, Osama bin Laden, were thought to be in hiding. The following year, they invaded Iraq, one of the principal enemies of Israel and believed to have links with al-Qa'eda.

The terrorists (Devil) responded equally quickly. In Bali on 11th September 2002, the first anniversary of the bombing of the World Trade Centre, they detonated bombs that killed over two hundred people, mainly Australians. Later, on 11th March 2004, they detonated a series of bombs in Madrid's underground rail system, killing 191 people and wounding many others. Then, on 7th July 2005, suicide bombers killed 52 people in London, and a fortnight later the same city was the target for another such team. This time they were unsuccessful. These attacks were intended to persuade governments to withdraw their forces from Iraq, and the Spanish government duly complied. This sign of weakness has encouraged other terrorists, hence the rest of the world is on a state of alert.

In the meantime, the USA-led coalition forces in Iraq toppled its dictatorial ruler, Saddam Hussein, and their counterparts in Afghanistan drove Osama bin Laden and his followers into neighbouring Pakistan. However, these successes have only served to increase the ferocity of the fighting and the determination of the terrorists.

But the most serious threat to Israel comes from Iran. It is not only the principal supporter of Islamist terrorist groups, but is also constructing facilities for the utilisation of nuclear power. Although the ruling Muslim clergy stoutly maintain they intend to use this power for peaceful purposes only, the West and Israel suspect otherwise, and the latter has declared it will launch pre-emptive strikes to destroy these facilities.

Are these suspicions justified? There is no proof that Iran's declared intent to utilise nuclear power for peaceful purposes is untrue. Indeed, the fact that fundamentalist Muslim clergy govern Iran adds credence to their claim!

The reason lies in the Muslim mindset, the key to which is complete acceptance that the Koran contains the wisdom of Allah, and cannot be questioned by Man. Therefore every Muslim's word and deed must accord with the Koran – the will of Allah. Since Allah is everywhere, Muslims believe they are always in His presence, which means they cannot tell lies. Therefore if the Muslim ruling clerics in Iran say they are developing nuclear power for peaceful purposes only, one ought to be able to take them at their word.

However, God's accompanying analysis to the game includes moves that He believes the Devil will make, and these, as we showed earlier, will induce Islamists to embrace violence in the belief that they are carrying out the will of Allah/God. Therefore the ruling clergy of Iran would conceal their true intent with regard to the development of nuclear power if they believed Allah/God had sanctioned such deception.

* * * * * * *

Everything points to the involvement of God and the Devil in developments in the Middle East. If the Devil is successful – scores another victory over God – then we will see fulfilment of the prophecy in Revelation that Armageddon will be the scene of the Final Conflict. Underlying this will be the supreme irony that the oldest racial conflict – between Arabs and Jews – will be the final conflict, and the trigger will be God's Chosen Race. This will indeed be a triumph for the Devil!

We dismiss this outcome, however, because Revelation was an account of the future that Jesus imparted to the Apostle John, and it ends with complete victory for God and Jesus. Therefore at some point in their game – the future – God gained a decisive advantage over the Devil, and we believe He has already initiated the strategy that secures Him this advantage.

The strategy is based on a number of considerations. Iran is not a major power and, but for its nuclear power programme, would receive little attention from the West. Iran is remote from Israel, and is cut off from Syria, its main ally and a neighbour of Israel, by Iraq, which the USA has democratised. Syria is in a state of turmoil, and it is unlikely that its president, Bashar al-Assad, will be in power for much longer. If, as seems likely, a Sunni Moslem becomes president – 70% of Syrians are Sunni – then Iran will lose its main ally.

Iran relies for technological and other forms of assistance on the USA's former Cold War opponents, Russia and China, but both have been hit hard by the recent global financial crisis. Russia requires Western finance and technology to exploit its vast deposits of oil and mineral wealth in Siberia, but it is institutionally corrupt, which has discouraged Western investment. China has remained communist, which means it has no welfare system to sustain its population through the crisis, and therefore relies on a vast inflow of wealth, but its overseas markets have been depressed by the crisis, and it has recorded its first trade deficit for twenty years.

Even without this, China's prospects are precarious. It needs to expand its economy by an annual rate of over 9% to meet the growing demands of its people, improve its infrastructure, cater for environmental concerns, and maintain the world's largest army, police force and communist party structure, yet the economy becomes overheated at 8.5% and has to be dampened down. Official government figures show it will only grow by 7.5% this year, which is not enough.

China will therefore have to introduce a welfare system, but this requires increases in taxation, and these inevitably lead to a parliamentary system where members debate the scope and rates of taxes. Eventually the debates will cover all areas of government policy, as they do in democracies.

This explains why the Chinese President, Wen Jiabao, recently intimated that China will have to follow in Russia's footsteps and become a democracy. It also explains why China (and Russia) is relying on the USA to lead it and the rest of the world out of economic recession.

These developments have unfolded with the strategic logic that characterises a game of chess between grandmasters. Noteworthy is the manner in which God fitted the global financial crisis into His plan, and turned to his advantage the USA-led invasion of Iraq, because the resulting democratisation of Iraq installed a democratic government on the borders of Iran and between Iran and Israel. Iran is now isolated and open to attack from Israel.

However, Israel cannot launch an attack on Iran without the permission of the USA, but the USA is democratic, and democratic governments cannot declare war, or embark on a course leading to war, without first winning the consent of the people. Governments always have opponents – free will finds opposing views on practically every policy – consequently the democratic process restrains the USA government.

Democracies are invariably Christian, and Christianity is an additional restraint on governments because, having abandoned militancy centuries ago, it seeks peaceful solutions to every problem. This explains why the US President, Barack Obama, is determined to bend Iran to his will by peaceful means, only permitting Israeli air strikes as a last resort.

With democracy the most widespread form of government, Christianity the foremost religion, and Iran effectively isolated, we have the best insurance policy against a war between Israel and Iran developing into the Final Conflict.

This timely combination of political and religious forces proves that Jesus' teachings contained a sub-text with political overtones that linked up with God's schedule. This link is therefore a precursor to the co-ordinated actions by God and Jesus detailed in Revelation that ultimately defeat the forces of the Devil. Consequently Man's future is writ in Revelation.

Chapter Two

The Prophecies in Revelation

Part 1

Jesus gave a glimpse of Man's future to the Apostle John, who faithfully recorded the details in the Book of Revelation. This is confirmed by the introductory words, "The Revelation of Jesus Christ, which God gave unto him, to show unto his servants things which must shortly come to pass," and is repeated at the end (Rev. 22.6) with the words, "These sayings are faithful and true: and the Lord God of the holy prophets sent his angel to shew unto his servants the things which must shortly be done."

However, this raises a key question: does Revelation set out the future that God had in mind for our forerunners, or was it revised to set out our future?

The answer to this question lies in the discovery by the Russian mathematician Nikolai Alexandrovich Morosov in March 1907 that passages in Revelation describe constellations that would appear over the island of Patmos on Sunday, 30th September 395 (Julian Year) as a solar eclipse was taking place.

Morosov says the day is named explicitly in Rev. 1.10: "I was in the Spirit on Sunday." The description of the sky is systematic, starting at the pole with a constellation named Throne (Ursa Minor): Rev. 4.2: "And a throne was set in heaven." The text goes on to mention the Milky Way and the signs of the zodiac that denote the four seasons: Leo, Taurus, Sagittarius, and Eagle (Aquarius): Rev. 4.6-7: "And before the throne there was a sea of glass like unto crystal: and in the midst of the throne and round about the throne were four beasts full of eyes before and behind. And the first beast was like a lion, and the second beast was like a calf, and the third beast had a face as a man, and the fourth beast was like a flying eagle."

Morosov interpreted the four horses as traditional metaphors for the planets Jupiter, Mars, Mercury, and Saturn. The constellations of Sagittarius, Perseus (Aries), Libra, and Scorpio were sitting on them: Rev. 6.2: "And I saw, and behold a white horse: and he that sat on him had a bow." Rev 6.4: "And there went out another horse that was red: and power was given to him that sat thereon to take peace from the earth, and that they should kill one another: and there was given unto him a great sword." Rev. 6.5: "And I beheld, and lo a black horse; and he that sat on him had a pair of balances in his hand." Rev. 6.8: "And I looked, and behold a pale horse: and his name that sat on him was Death, and Hell followed with him."

The Sun and Moon were named explicitly in Rev. 12.1, and Virgo is implicit because she the only female in the zodiac: "And there appeared a great wonder in heaven: a woman clothed with the sun, and the moon under her feet, and upon her head a crown of twelve stars."

Venus, the symbol of female eroticism, unites with the red star Antares (Anti-Mars) in the constellation of Scorpio, and this is recorded in Rev. 17.3-4: "and I saw a woman sit upon a scarlet coloured beast… And the woman was arrayed in purple and scarlet colour, and decked with gold and precious stones and pearls, having a golden cup in her hand full of abominations and filthiness of her fornication."

Morosov worked back through the Saros cycle of eclipses and took into account Earth's rate of precession. Recently his calculations were checked by the planetarium programme Yoursky and, after allowance was made for changes in Earth's precession since 395, were found to be correct. Thus there can be no doubt that Revelation exactly predicted the constellations in the sky as a solar eclipse was about to take place at 3.00 p.m. on the Julian date of 30th September 395.

This prediction would have been impossible in our forerunner's day, because eclipses are only brought about by the movements of stars and planets in our universe, therefore Revelation must be God's revised analysis, and is intended to show how He believes events will unfold after we rejoin His schedule on 20th August 1953.

However, God's schedule runs concurrently on four different time-scales: astronomical (tidying up the universe after the Big Bang, laying out the Solar System), geological (designing Earth, creating life), historical (the time-line in the Great Pyramid), and in the future (Man exploring space, contacting other life-forms, and restoring the object God had designed but which was destroyed by the Big Bang), consequently Revelation runs concurrently on these time-scales.

Thus modern scholars, accepting the traditional view that Revelation was written between A.D. 68 and 95, have taken the "shortly come to pass" time-scale to mean the contents must be viewed in the context of the first century. Revelation then becomes an address to seven Christian communities in Asia Minor, warning them not to conform to Greco-Roman society because it is beastly, demonic and subject to divine judgement.[28]

However, Revelation consists of four great dramatic events, and these unfold over a much longer period of time. There is increasing hostility followed by punishment and the final extermination of the enemies of God and Jesus.

---

28 Pope Benedict XVI also accepts this view. During a discussion concerning Revelation on 23rd August 2006, he said, "The seer of Patmos, identified with the apostle [John], is granted a series of visions meant to reassure the Christians of Asia amid the persecutions and trials at the end of the first century."

Thus John's first vision, covered in Rev. 8.2-9,21; 11.1-4; 12.1-13.18, is of the Three Woes – plagues sounded by seven Trumpets – and shows how, notwithstanding divine warnings and repeated catastrophes, the unbelievers persist in their lack of repentance. The vision culminates in the war of the Dragon against the Woman and her child, and the rise of the Two Beasts, symbolising the climax of moral perversion in the history of mankind. In the second vision, the plagues of the Seven Bowls (Rev. 16.1-17, 18) are poured out over the worshippers of the Beast and bring about the fall of Great Babylon. In both visions, the agents of God are angels.

In the third vision, Jesus appears, riding a white horse and defeating his enemies. He reigns for a thousand years (millennium), after which the Devil (Satan) is released for a short while, but, following the defeat of his last abortive rebellion, is cast into the Lake of Fire (Rev. 19.11-20.10). The last vision depicts the Great White Throne, the resurrection of the dead, and the new Jerusalem with all its heavenly splendour and bliss (Rev. 20.11-22.5).

Each vision contains so many figurative allusions and other forms of embroidery that one can readily understand why many scholars consider Revelation to have no intrinsic value, and some believe it does not belong in the Bible. However, when we remove the embellishments the picture that emerges is one showing God and Jesus relentlessly co-ordinating their actions and those of their followers to defeat the Devil and allow Man to take his rightful place beside God in Heaven.

This must have been the triumph God had in mind for our forerunners, but which was destroyed by the Big Bang, hence it is the victory He predicts for us.

However, God could not have predicted events after 20th August 1953 because these did not occur in our forerunners' day, therefore His forecast can be upset. We might bring about the Battle of Armageddon in circumstances other than those in which He expects to emerge victorious. Nevertheless, Christianity's power for peace and the dominance of democracy appear to be capable of averting the Final Conflict on this time-scale, as we showed in the previous chapter. Since these forces arise from the teachings of Jesus, it is likely that God took them into account when revising Revelation.

Part 2

Having shown that God's prediction is unlikely to be upset on the historical time-scale and in the near future, we now have to see if it holds true on the geological time-scale. We shall therefore examine various factors that could upset His calculations.

Experts predict Man is facing four crises: a shortage of energy supplies and climate change induced by excessive emissions of carbon dioxide and global warming. These crises bear all the hall-marks of the nightmarish figures in Revelation – the Four Horsemen of the Apocalypse – which between them represent war, famine, pestilence, and death. Since many believe future wars will be fought over energy and water supplies, the horsemen convey a clear warning for the future.

God created a natural environment that was perfectly suited for Man's needs, but it was finely balanced, and experts believe Man has upset the balance. Thousands of species become extinct each year, and many place the blame on changes Man has made to the environment. These changes, it is claimed, affect the climate by causing global warming, which has a disastrous effect on many forms of life. However, we shall show that the root cause of global warming cannot be laid at Man's door, and the extinction of these species is not the global tragedy that many portray.

The extinction of a species creates a gap in the food-chain. This means a particular creature has no predator, or a type of vegetation goes uneaten. Such a gap cannot exist for long, because every species has to eat. Consequently a species closely related to the one that has become extinct evolves until it is able to feed on the prey or vegetation, thereby closing the gap in the food-chain. This creates a species bearing the characteristics both of its original design and that of the extinct variety, and we believe this is one of the reasons why most species of plants and animals have many varieties.

Given that God devised the laws of Nature and engineered two mass extinctions to pave the way for the introduction of Man, we arrive at a fundamental law of Nature: mass extinctions lead to new life-forms, which constitutes progress.

* * * * * * *

Man has been blamed for global warming, because it is believed to result from emissions of carbon dioxide that are released when he burns fossil fuels in industrial processes and transportation. However, these fuels were created by natural chemical reactions on decaying plant material, hence they are part of the environment God created for us. Therefore He meant us to make full use of them. If our exploitation of these fuels has reached the point at which they are having an adverse effect on other aspects of God's design, then He must have devised a means of making them 'clean'. It should therefore come as no surprise that scientists have recently discovered the technology for burning coal 'cleanly'.

This means we have to look elsewhere for the cause of global warming.

The real reason for global warming is to reduce the amount of ice that has accumulated around the South Pole (Antarctica). Whereas people have watched the disappearance of ice around this pole (and the North Pole) with mounting dread, we believe it is a necessary correction!

Earth is tilted away from the Sun, and in order to maintain the correct angle of tilt – it is essential for life – there must only be a certain amount of ice at the poles. We showed on p. 30 that movements of the tectonic plates resulted in Antarctica providing the perfect counterweight to the landmasses that had accumulated around the North Pole, but the balance has now been lost. Far too much ice has accumulated around the South Pole, with the result that the North Pole has been forced nearer the Sun. This explains why ice in this region has started to melt. The reduction of ice increases the imbalance with Antarctica, and this has a two-fold effect: it accelerates the movement of the North Pole towards the Sun, and Antarctica swings further away. This makes Antarctica colder, more ice-laden, and further out of balance with the North Pole. It is the start of a vicious spiral.

However, Professor Hugh Auchincloss Brown, in his *Cataclysms of the Earth* (1967), sketched out an even worse scenario. Certain cataclysms of the past have been caused when the poles of figure (magnetic) move away from the poles of spin (axial), causing Earth to wobble on its axis until it realigns and spins again like a top. Brown noted that Earth has been rotating on its present axis for about 7,000 years, causing Antarctica to increase its weight to 19 quadrillion tons. If it continued to increase at the same rate, Brown calculated that by the end of the twentieth century 98% of the world's permanent ice would be weighing down the southern polar region. Eventually the burden would become so great that it would unbalance Earth's axis, causing continents to rift and drift. The ice of Antarctica would melt, flooding the world with a new water level 300 feet higher than it is at present. This level of water would drown all ports and lowlands.

The only way to prevent both scenarios is to achieve a huge reduction in the amount of ice at the South Pole. The North Pole will then move away from the Sun, and ice in this region will start to freeze. Eventually the stability that once existed will be restored.

This task is far beyond Man's capability, but the evidence of melting ice in Antarctica shows that Nature has not only begun the task, but is equal to it. In 1985 a huge hole suddenly appeared in the ozone layer and exposed the entire Antarctic continent to the Sun's rays, enabling them to focus like a laser beam on the excess ice and slice it off. In 2002 the Antarctic Peninsula's Larsen-B ice shelf sheared off. Between 28th February and 8th March 2008, about 220 square miles of ice from the Wilkins Ice Shelf fell away, leaving the remaining 5,800 square miles of ice shelf holding on by a 'thread' of ice only 4 miles wide. The thread snapped on 5th April 2009.

The timing of this form of salvation is too perfect to be accidental. Furthermore, it utilises the power output of the Sun, which God had calculated would present no threat to us. It is therefore further proof that God installed various mechanisms in Earth and the Solar System, the purpose of which was to provide Man with the right environment for as long as he needs it.

* * * * * * *

Our analysis shows God foresaw these four crises because He devised the means whereby certain are averted, others work out to our advantage, and He has put in place the mechanism for dealing with global warming, consequently these crises do not upset the geological time-scale of His schedule.

This brings us to events that will unfold on an astronomical time-scale. Key events in Revelation fit events that happened to Man's forerunners before Time began. For example, God consigns the Devil to imprisonment in the Pit because of the rôle that he played in the Battle of Armageddon, but before Time began the Devil had succeeded in tempting Man's forerunners to bring about the Big Bang and destroy the object God had designed, so we may assume this offence carried the same punishment.

Further proof that Armageddon occurs at the beginning and end of Time is the fact that the 16th September 1936 in the Great Pyramid's time-line marks the end of the 'Veil of Tribulation and Humility' and the entrance to the Hall of Judgement in our forerunners' day, but also heralds the Age of Aquarius, and equates to the "sounding of the

Seventh Trumpet" in Revelation that marks the beginning of the "times of the end" and the dawning of a 'New Order of the Ages'.

The 'New Order of the Ages' arrived in 2001, and the time-line in the Great Pyramid expired at midnight 22nd September 2001. This date, we believe, refers to the Big Bang (see p. 155), hence Revelation simultaneously predicts a new age and refers to the event that began Time!

God did not release the Devil until He had endowed Adam and Eve with free will, for this enabled their thoughts to scan good and evil, hence the Devil's term of imprisonment spanned the period during which stars and galaxies formed, God created the Solar System, designed Earth's structure, created the right environment for Man, and finally introduced Man. Since the wording of the indictment against the Devil given in Revelation 20.2 can be applied both to his "deceit" of Man and that of our forerunners, the thousand-year term of imprisonment must be figurative.

* * * * * * *

Since the time-frame of Revelation incorporates events at the beginning and end of Time, Revelation must contain a code Jesus devised to conceal from us events in our future that operate on an astronomical time-scale and are of astronomical proportions. The concealment was necessary for the same reason that his teachings – and God's schedule – had to be encoded.

Revelation culminates in the Battle of Armageddon, consequently this battle must arise from forces beyond our control. This can only mean it was brought about by conflicting universal forces, and this brings God and the Devil into the equation.

We showed how God moved to create our world and life itself, but the moment He bestowed on Man free will, He effectively released the Devil, and the Devil has to destroy Man. What forces can the Devil utilise to achieve this end?

The only force at the Devil's disposal is Man's free will, because it allows us to contemplate evil, consequently the Devil can only triumph if we respond badly to events. It is in this light that we have to analyse astronomical events and their repercussions, as we show in the following chapters.

CHAPTER THREE

THREATS TO MAN FROM OUTER SPACE

GOD DESIGNED THE SOLAR System in such a manner that it protected Earth, but could certain of its dynamics threaten Man? We examined this possibility in *God Designs the Solar System*, but only insofar as it related to Earth's positioning and formation. The installation of Man starts a new chapter.

For example, astronomers had long known that on 10th March 1982, the planets Mercury, Venus, Earth, Mars, Jupiter, Saturn, and Pluto would align on the same side of the Sun within an arc 95° wide, and some scientists predicted this would create a number of catastrophes, including an earthquake along the San Andreas Fault. During Earth's formation this would not have been a problem, but now this fault runs through some of the most heavily populated towns and cities in California.

However, the catastrophes did not occur. The only difference was fractionally higher tides – 40 micrometers – that caused no inconvenience.

The reason the alignment had little effect is that the gravitational force of the planets on Earth's crust is minimal even at their closest approach. Since this is the worst-case scenario for planetary alignment, mankind has nothing to fear from this feature of the Solar System. God's layout withstands this test.

Scientists have also applied the alignment to the Sun, to see how it affects the Sun's rotation and hence the speed/strength of solar winds. These winds are known to affect the weather on Earth, and changes to the atmosphere alter the speed of Earth's rotation. However, measurements have shown that the alignment would have little effect on the Sun.

The minimal effect of planetary alignment is because the mass of the planets, taken as a whole, is insignificant compared to the mass of the Sun. The Sun comprises 99.9% of the mass of the Solar System. It is 300,000 times more massive than Earth and 1,000 times more massive than Jupiter, therefore the main threats to Earth must originate from within the Sun.

On 15th March 2012, the surface of the Sun exploded, unleashing two solar flares – enormous bursts of hot plasma – that headed straight towards Earth, the fastest travelling at 1,300 miles per second. The force of these flares was more than Earth's magnetic shield could withstand, and so they covered Earth's atmosphere.

The result was a beautiful display of auroral effects. Solar flares are not a threat to life, but they are extremely inconvenient now that Man has launched satellites into the upper atmosphere. These satellites transmit data to Earth in the form of electromagnetic signals, consequently when the superfast, superhot magnetised solar plasma slammed into the atmosphere, it induced electrical currents that interfered with the signals from the satellites. The upper atmosphere became a no-go area for aviation because of the risk of navigational havoc and exposure to radiation. Polar flights had to be rerouted.

Another effect of the plasma was to heat the lower layers of the atmosphere, causing gases to expand, become lighter, and rise into the layers of the atmosphere where satellites orbit. These layers become denser, upsetting the orbits of satellites. In 1979 the increased density caused Skylab to crash to Earth.

The satellites are vital for linking Man on a global scale because they provide him with sat-nav, communications, radio and television. They integrate Man by transcending racial and political differences. They are crucial if Man is to achieve worldwide peace and harmony in accordance with God's schedule.

Solar flares are also a threat to manned expeditions to Mars, the Moon and other planets. Energetic protons pass through the human body, causing biochemical damage, and therefore represent a threat to astronauts during interplanetary travel.

The exploration of space is the next stage of God's schedule, therefore it is no accident that scientists are close to neutralising the effects of solar flares. They discovered that flares originate from plasma bubbles in the Sun's core rising to the surface. Their magnetic fields project from the surface in a series of loops – solar arcades – that constitute lines of magnetic force. These lines of force quickly reconnect into a low arcade of loops, leaving a helix of the magnetic field unconnected to the rest of the arcade. The process of magnetic reconnection releases energy in the form of particle acceleration. The unconnected magnetic helical field and the plasma it contains are violently expanded outward as a solar flare.

The plasma bubbles can be detected by sound waves, because sound travels faster through the bubbles than through the churning mass of plasma, consequently scientists have devised instruments that listen to the Sun. These, together with satellites positioned to intercept solar flares and transmit their speed/direction, give satellite operators time to reposition their satellites and reschedule manned flights.

They will also give operators of national grids time to neutralise another effect of solar flares. In 1989 and again in 2003 solar flares earthed, producing electromagnetic currents that overloaded power systems. In the earlier instance, the city of Quebec was blacked out within 92 seconds, and it was nine hours before power was restored. In the later case, much of Sweden and Africa were blacked out.

Operators now realise that if they are given early warning of the direction of a solar flare, they can switch on every transformer in target areas and dissipate the flare's energy, thus avoiding black outs.

With these protections against solar flares, and Earth's magnetic shield – which reaches 40,000 miles into space – protecting everyone and everything from solar winds, there can be no doubt that God selected the Sun to be the star in our Solar System because its power output was no great threat to Man.

This does not mean, however, that the Sun's power does not present us with challenges. Solar flares and solar winds are minor matters compared to other effects that we shall have to overcome. Our climate derives from the power of the Sun, but it interacts with dynamics that originate on Earth, and this interaction has recently brought about ominous changes in the climate. We have already examined the short-term effects of climate change, but scientists have begun to take note of a longer-term change that is potentially far more serious. We shall examine this threat in the following chapter.

CHAPTER FOUR

THE THREAT TO MAN FROM ICE AGES

Part 1

ICE IS AN EVER-PRESENT feature of Earth's surface. It exists not only at the poles but also on the tops of mountains and at high altitudes generally. The weight of ice is beyond measure, and when this weight/mass is transformed into energy – forward movement – then it is an irresistible force that gouges the terrain. This has the benefit of removing features that would otherwise hinder Man's progress, and in this respect it complements the action of rainfall and rivers, but it has one very bad effect: it reflects sunlight. The more ice on the surface, the colder the temperature, and unless the ice retreats, Earth suffers an ice age.

Ice ages have occurred repeatedly in Earth's history, and this is due, according to the Yugoslav mathematician Milutin Milankovic, to a combination of factors relating to Earth's orbit, angle of tilt and precession.

Earth's orbit is elliptical, and every 94,000 years reaches its furthest position (aphelion) from the Sun. Earth's angle of tilt varies between 22° and 24° every 41,000 years, and Earth precesses every 25,825.5 years. When these cycles converge, sunlight is redistributed and the seasons change, creating the basic conditions for an ice age: long-continued precipitation in the form of snow, and temperatures so low that summer melting is minimal, allowing snowfields to carry over from year to year and glaciers to form.

Every factor that contributes to the underlying causes of ice ages relates to Earth's positioning and formation, as well as the general layout of the Solar System. These factors God had calculated to perfection, consequently He deliberately incorporated ice ages into Earth's dynamics.

The reason He did so is revealed by the Pleistocene ice age. This occurred 10,000 years ago and covered 10% of Earth, but it wiped out many fearsome creatures that were a threat to Man.

This means ice ages are meant to remove landscape features and other factors that impede Man's progress, enabling him to make fresh starts in improved settings.

Consequently we must expect ice ages in the future, and the question is whether or not God had planned this far ahead. If He did, then ice ages will be to our benefit. If not, then the Devil can utilise them to threaten Man's existence.

The conditions for another ice age already exist. From 1850 to 1950 most of the world's glaciers have been shrinking, hence sea level has been rising. Furthermore, during the past sixty years Arctic ice has been melting. If and when it completely melts, the Arctic will be warmed by the Gulf Stream, recreating the conditions that, according to the Ewing-Donn Hypothesis, caused the Pleistocene ice age.

According to this theory, before the Pleistocene epoch, the Pacific Ocean spread over the north polar regions, making them much warmer than they are now. At this time, the present arctic geographic areas were where the North Pacific is now. Then came a drift of Earth's crust that placed North America, Siberia and the Arctic Ocean in their present positions. The water of the Arctic Ocean at this time was warm, and was kept warm by the inflow of the Gulf Stream from the Atlantic. The warm arctic water evaporated and provided heavy snowfalls in northern

America, Europe and Siberia. This caused the Pleistocene glaciation of these areas. The glaciation stopped because the glacial ice lowered sea level about 300 feet, and the Gulf Stream could not cross the high sills or ridges that separated the basins of the Arctic and North Atlantic oceans. Without the warm Atlantic water, the Arctic froze over, ending the supply of water for further snowfall.

When the Arctic ice completely melts, the water can be warmed by the Gulf Stream, because it can once again cross the barrier sills. This will supply water for evaporation, snowfall and renewed glaciation on all borders of the ocean.

Another theory is based on the effect of warm and cold ocean currents on the climate of the continents. The warm Gulf Stream washes the north coast of South America, moves through the Caribbean Sea and the Gulf of Mexico, and then crosses the North Atlantic to warm Western Europe. If the Isthmus of Panama subsided a few hundred feet, then there would be no true Gulf Stream, for warm water from the Atlantic would be driven by Trade Winds into the Pacific. The North Atlantic water would be much colder, as would the countries of Western Europe formerly warmed by the Gulf Stream.

This scenario is an echo of stories of the "Lost Continent of Atlantis", which is supposed to have existed between Europe and North America. Studies through soundings and samplings by coring tubes of the mid-Atlantic Ridge, which extends south from Iceland to 20° north latitude, indicate that it was once a land mass. If so, then all of Western Europe would have been very much colder until Atlantis sunk, which shows how changes in the circulation of ocean water can help to bring about an ice age.

The threat could become reality for the UK because the melting of glaciers in Greenland could terminate the Gulf Stream before it reaches this country. Glaciers are composed of fresh water, and each melting pours millions of tons of ice-cold fresh water into the North Atlantic. This acts as a barrier that the warm salt-laden Gulf Stream cannot cross, hence it descends the 'wall' of fresh water until it reaches the sea-bed and returns to the Gulf. This would deprive the UK of its warm summer and prolong its winter, which would turn very much colder.

Another theory is that changes in solar radiation create ice ages. Studies of sunspots, which are violent eruptions in the Sun's atmosphere, reveal great annual and periodic variations in the amount of heat received by Earth from the Sun. During maximum sunspot activity, the Sun radiates more than its normal amount of heat, which causes greater circulation of Earth's atmosphere, with greater than normal cloudiness and precipitation. Because the clouds intercept the Sun's rays, the land surface receives less than normal heat. This ought not to cause an ice age, but it has been suggested that there may be very long cycles, perhaps thousands of years in duration, when the Sun radiates more or less than normal heat.

Sir George Simpson, a British meteorologist, believes this is the explanation for the four stages of Pleistocene glaciation. He visualises two very long cycles of greater than normal radiation. Towards maximum radiation in the first cycle, increased heat caused increased activity in Earth's atmosphere, great evaporation, great snowfall, and the first stage of an ice age. At the peak, Earth itself began to warm up until the heat became so great that the glaciers melted, giving an interglacial stage. As radiation decreased, conditions came to resemble those of the first glaciation, and a second glacial stage occurred. This ended when the cycle of radiation reached a minimum, because atmospheric circulation, evaporation and snowfall decreased, and the glaciers wasted away for lack of snow.

Part 3

The power of the Sun is the common factor in the causes of ice ages, either directly – solar radiation, sunspot activity – or through its effect on Earth's climate. In addition to this, the Sun's power is a key factor in global warming, one result of which is increased water levels. Given that God had taken every aspect of the Sun's power into account before finalising the layout of the Solar System (particularly Earth's positioning), He must have prepared a resource that enables us to avert these impending disasters.

The overall effect of these threats is to render uninhabitable large areas of Earth's surface for geologically long periods of time. We shall therefore have to seek refuge, and the only refuge is the interior. Consequently Earth's mantle will have to live up to its name and cover or conceal us from hostile elements.

This means we will have to construct underground towns and cities. It will be a huge and enormously expensive task, but we appear to have no choice. As compensation, however, underground complexes have many advantages over those on the surface. They are weather-proof, the atmosphere can be computer-controlled to produce optimum air-conditioning, and properties can incorporate state-of-the art features.

The complexes will have to be linked by road and rail systems. These will be computer-controlled to produce the best and safest driving conditions. Compare that with the thousands of motorists' lives lost each year due to dangerous weather conditions!

At present express trains travel overground and their average speed is less than a hundred miles an hour, whereas electrically-powered underground inter-city/inter-continental rail links should achieve far greater speeds. The trains can be gradually accelerated to speeds of thousands of mph. by placing electric magnets along their routes. This system already operates in the Large Haydron Collider to accelerate particles close to the speed of light, so it merely needs to be adapted to meet the requirements of underground rail systems. Likewise a team of engineers demonstrated in a recent (2010) programme on the *Discovery* channel the feasibility of constructing a tunnel for high-speed trains under the Atlantic Ocean that would link the UK and USA.

Underground road and rail systems provide a much safer and faster means of transporting people and freight anywhere in the world. The systems will link everyone, so an essential precondition is political, social and economic harmony. But since this is the precondition we have to achieve before we can proceed to the next stage of God's schedule, living underground accords with His schedule. This explains why the technological and engineering skills necessary to construct high-speed underground railways have recently been discovered.

* * * * * * *

It therefore comes as no surprise that God has catered for our needs underground, firstly by providing us with a limitless source of underground heat and energy. The source is the molten rock surrounding Earth's iron core. We showed that God designed the core to serve a multitude of purposes, so our discovery of yet another use for it amply testifies to His extraordinary foresight.

Heat and energy generated from molten rock is termed geo-thermal energy, and because it originates from fundamental features of Earth's interior, it will be present for as long as Earth exists. It is therefore a perpetual source of power.

Earth's interior consists of a crust about 20-35 miles thick, and this is where underground complexes will be situated. The crust is much thinner than the layer beneath – the mantle – which stretches down about 1,800 miles to the molten core. The mantle provides the source of molten hot rock and gases (magma) that erupt in volcanic activity. The heat comes from the radioactive decay of materials within the core. The heat is so intense that it can melt rock in the mantle. The hot rock may produce pockets of heat near the surface that can interact with water to form steam or hot water. Because the system is usually confined, the fluids are often at high pressure and at temperatures above the boiling point of water.

Geothermal features usually occur in volcanic regions at the boundaries of Earth's crustal plates, consequently geothermal heat/energy is only used in a few countries, such as Iceland, Italy and New Zealand, that have a high incidence of volcanic activity. The chief drawbacks to greater exploitation are the cost of extraction and Man's belief that he is meant to live on the surface. Once he realises that his future lies in towns and cities underground, then the cost has to be met, and he will find that geo-thermal sources supply all his energy requirements. God created Earth to fulfil our needs for as long as we exist, therefore geothermal energy will be accessible and not have any significant environmental drawbacks.

Another essential substance for sustaining life in the underground complexes is water. Since the populations will be huge, the supply of water has to be practically limitless. The complexes will also be spread throughout Earth's crust, and therefore the supply has to be equally widespread. God, however, has catered for both requirements!

Wherever the complexes are situated, they can easily be connected to desalination plants in seas and oceans, because these cover 70% of Earth's surface. By this means people – and all forms of life – are certain of receiving adequate supplies of fresh water. Before returning water to the seas and oceans, it can be resalinated using the salt that had been extracted. This cycle ensures that water is perpetual and sustains life everywhere.

The cycle is only possible because liquid water is present in large quantities over most of Earth's surface. Since Earth is unique in this respect, its seas/oceans should be regarded as design features that God installed, and scientists have discovered that they perform a host of vital functions, including providing the main engine that powers Earth's climate. We have now discovered a completely new use for them, but it is one that God must have foreseen at an early state of Earth's formation.

Water itself has unique properties that could only have been infused by design, therefore God intended us to make use of water's uniqueness and its dispersal worldwide. We have done so in many different ways, and now we have found another use for them – one that fits so neatly into God's schedule that He must have intended us to live underground.

People living underground have to be fed. Given that much of Earth's surface currently devoted to agriculture may in due course no longer be able to do so, it cannot be coincidental that Man has recently made great strides in the development and cultivation of genetically-modified (GM) crops. Certain varieties already produce far greater yields than their natural counterparts, and do so in the most inhospitable regions.

To a certain extent Man is merely copying Nature, because evolution entails genetic modifications, but there is a crucial difference. Natural evolution maintains the balance that is essential in our environment, whereas GM crops designed by Man are artificial and, if introduced into the environment, may upset or destroy the balance. This point has been brought home to scientists who are conducting research into GM crops, and now they are seeking to develop crops that meet Man's needs and harmonise with Nature.

The necessity to take such precautions with GM crops shows the fineness of the balance in Nature. The balance is brought about by the activities of billions of organisms and millions of species of plants, insects and creatures, none of which have any concept of the balance they create, hence it arises only because God, at the outset, laid down the laws of Nature.

Laws have to adapt to changing conditions, and changes are forcing us to develop GM crops. God's schedule also requires us to develop these crops for life underground, therefore we will in due course discover the means by which they can be produced and harmonise with Nature. The timing for our acquisition of this knowledge depends – as always – on God's schedule.

Chapter Five

The Threat To Man From Volcanic Activity

Part 1

God provided us with the resources to meet the threats posed by ice ages and rising water levels. In addition, once we begin to drain the heat/energy within magma chambers, we reduce the intensity of another impending global threat: volcanic activity.

This threat recently came to the fore with the eruption of Eyjafjallajokull in Iceland. The eruption began on 14th April 2010, and created a dense cloud of volcanic ash that drifted across the UK, Scandinavia and much of Europe. The cloud posed such a serious threat to air traffic that planes were grounded and hundreds of thousands of passengers were left stranded.

But this eruption was small in comparison with the previous eruption of Eyjafjallajokull in 1823, which lasted for over a year, and this was small in comparison with overall volcanic activity in Iceland. Volcanologists estimate that there are thirty active volcanic systems on the island, and the reason is that it sits on a 'mantle plume', a rising column of abnormally hot molten rock originating at the edge of Earth's core.

In the past ten years, volcanologists have noticed increased disturbances below Iceland that suggest the volcanic systems are entering a more active phase. The last time Iceland had a major eruption was in 1783. Laki, a fissure in the Grimsvotn volcano system, suddenly burst open and threw up fountains of lava and clouds of ash for eight months. The eruption ejected 3.6 cubic miles of material compared to the fraction of a cubic mile ejected by Eyjafallajokull.

On the volcanicity explosive index (VEI), which measures the amount of material ejected, the height of the eruption, and its duration, Laki is judged to have scored six. That compares with a score of four for the Mount St. Helens eruption in 1980, and five or six for Mount Pinatubo's eruption in 1991.

The eruption of Mount St. Helens is regarded as a one-in-10-year event, Mount Pinatubo as a one-in-50-year event, and Laki as a one-in-100-year event. These are small, however, compared with the eruption of Tambora in 1815, which was one of the deadliest eruptions in recorded history. It killed over 70,000 people, achieved a seven rating on the VEI, and is regarded as a one-in-1,000-year event.

But this is small compared to the eruptions of supervolcanoes! These are one-in-100,000-year events. Over 625 cubic miles of material are blasted into the air on average, and the resulting cloud of ash/gas chills Earth for years. The last occasion on which a supervolcano erupted was 74,000 years ago, when Toba, on the Indonesian island of Sumatra, ejected 1,562 cubic miles of magma, nearly twice the volume of Mount Everest. The resulting cloud of volcanic ash was 300 times greater than that produced by Tambora in 1815.

Toba was over 5,000 times the explosive force of Mount St. Helens, and scores eight on the VEI, but is dwarfed by the Fish Canyon Tuff Event in Colorado 28 million years ago, which ejected over 3,000 cubic miles of magma.

* * * * * * *

Possible contenders for the next supervolcanic eruption are the Phlegrean fields volcano west of Naples and Lake Taupo in New Zealand, but most experts believe the next to erupt will be the supervolcano under Yellowstone Park in Wyoming, USA.

Its magma chamber is vast – 50 miles long, 25 miles wide, and 5 miles deep, sufficient to contain 6,250 cubic miles of magma. The gas emitted by the magma is being compressed against the roof of the chamber by rising magma, and the pressure is becoming intolerable. One slight weakness in the ground above or around the chamber will be sufficient to allow the gas to escape, and the ensuing eruption will have unimaginable force. The effect on the USA and the whole of North America will be catastrophic, but the rest of the world will also suffer, owing to the vast amount of ash and gas hurled into the atmosphere.

Supervolcanic eruptions are linked with mass extinctions, such as the Permian extinction 250 million years ago, but this means they fit in with God's schedule (see p. 18). Since we have no way of avoiding the next eruption, this must also be part of God's plan. He must therefore have provided us with the necessary resources to sustain us.

It must be possible to tap into the magma and draw off the gas. It cannot be part of God's plan to destroy the USA because it plays a vital rôle in His schedule (see p. 174), and our suggestion will ease the pressure and avert an eruption. Aside from saving the USA and the rest of the world from a cataclysm, it will also provide the USA with an abundant, natural source of energy. The USA needs such a source, because its natural supplies of oil and gas are becoming increasingly difficult to extract.

Geologists define Yellowstone Park as a caldera. This is a geological feature formed when the emptying of magma from the chamber causes the volcano to collapse, resulting in the formation of a depression. Calderas often become covered by water that forms a lake, but although this gives an outward appearance of calm, disturbances are happening underground. Magma rises through fissures to fill the chamber, setting the stage for a fresh eruption.

Clearly it is difficult for scientists to detect supervolcanoes that are simmering, but there are a number of likely areas: Indonesia, the Philippines, several Central American countries, the Andes, Japan, the Kamchatka peninsula in eastern Russia, and Europe (the area around Kos and Nisyros in the Aegean sea). Many of these regions have caldera lakes, and another excellent example is Crater Lake in Oregon, formed when Mount Mazama erupted about 6,000 years ago. This beautiful, nearly circular lake is 1,995 feet deep, the seventh deepest in the world.

* * * * * * *

The Katla caldera in Iceland is showing alarming signs of activity. This is indicative of an impending eruption, because Katla has erupted on average every 60 years, but has not had a significant eruption since 1918. Both Katla and Eyjafallajokull belong to the same volcanic system, Grimsvotn, which is why the eruptions of Eyjafallajokull in 1821-3 and 1612 were followed within months by eruptions of Katla. Judged by this, a Katla eruption is long overdue – and Katla is far larger than Eyjafallajokull.

In July 2011, Katla's ice cap was shattered by a burst of water from beneath, indicating that an extra pulse of heat had reached the base of the ice. Since then there have been erratic movements of the surface of the volcano, measured by precise GPS instruments, and bursts of high earthquake activity beneath Katla's caldera. These observations imply that magma has risen to shallower depths.

Katla's eruption in 1918 produced five times as much ash as the eruption of Eyjafallajokull in 2010. A major eruption could result in large parts of Iceland being flooded as snow and ice melt, significant poisoning of Icelandic agriculture, destruction of property, and the grounding of aircraft across Europe.

Part 2

A volcanic eruption can eject enough material to have a cooling effect on the global climate. A precedent for this is the 1783-4 eruption of Laki, which is part of the same volcanic system (Grimsvotn) as Katla and Eyjafallajokull. The Laki eruption was huge, as we mentioned earlier, but its worst feature was a cloud of ash containing sulphur dioxide, a gas that is poisonous and reflects sunlight. Temperatures across the northern hemisphere fell by up to 3° Centigrade, the gas killed over half of Iceland's livestock population, and caused a famine that wiped out about a quarter of Iceland's human population. As the cloud drifted south, the sulphur dioxide caused a thick haze to spread across Western Europe, resulting in thousands of deaths throughout 1783 and 1784. Further afield the effects were also severe. There is evidence that the Laki eruption may have caused the failure of the rice harvest in Japan, and weakened the African/Indian monsoon circulation.

Large eruptions such as this occur only every few hundred years in Iceland, but the potential for danger is significant. Even if deaths from famine are less likely today, a recent study of the potential effects of air pollution caused by such an eruption suggested fatalities in Europe would range from 52,000 to 228,000.

Meanwhile nearby Hekla has erupted about once every 10 years in recent times, with the last being in 2000. Similarly, volcanoes beneath the largest ice cap, Vatnajokull, are entering a period of increased volcanic activity – the peak of a 140-year cycle.

This trend is being accelerated by global warming. Vatnajokull has lost an estimated 400 billion tons of ice since the end of the 19th century, which has reduced the pressure on the hot mantle material beneath the crust, and led to increased magma generation. At the end of the last ice age, this same effect led to eruption rates some 30 times higher than at present. The current rate of ice loss is much lower, but we can still expect the formation of extra magma equivalent to that which erupted from Eyjafallajokull in 2010 every ten years or so.

Part 3

The link between global warming and increased volcanic activity is both ominous and surprising. Ominous because both are unavoidable – as we pointed out earlier, God considers global warming to be necessary so as to reduce the amount of ice that has accumulated around the North and South Poles – and surprising because the resulting volcanic activity does enormous damage and therefore seems to be counter to God's plan. However, God has seen much further ahead. Volcanic eruptions generate ash clouds that cool Earth's atmosphere and bring on ice ages that end global warming and change Earth's landscape for the better.

Consequently this sequence of events – global warming, increased volcanic activity, ice ages – constitutes a cycle spanning thousands of years that God devised and which eventually accelerates our rate of progress. This means we cannot avoid the next cycle, and indeed the conditions for another ice age already exist, partly for reasons given in the previous chapter and also because of increased volcanic activity.

The problem facing scientists is that they do not know when this increased activity will lead to full-scale eruptions. Studies indicate that the time lag between generation and eruption could be as much as a few hundred years. In the meantime the shrinking of ice caps on volcanoes is causing stress changes in the crust that may reduce the capture of magma on its way up.

We believe God's plan is to delay widespread eruptions until global warming has sufficiently reduced the ice around the poles that balance is restored, and Antarctica is once again the perfect counterweight to the landmasses around the Arctic Circle. This could take hundreds of years, so our theory fits in with scientific studies.

This means God has given scientists enough time to improve the instrumentation for eruption prediction, and this will enable them to devise better plans for dealing with the effects of eruptions, including the threats to agriculture and air travel.

To this end a group of scientists at the Delft University of Technology, led by Professor Andrew Hooper, are working with the University of Iceland and others to develop more accurate models of volcanic plumbing systems. Using GPS receivers, satellite-borne radar, and advanced algorithms, they have been able to track the movements of magma and create maps of magma storage.

Just as importantly, scientists are thoroughly assessing the risks associated with the largest Icelandic eruptions, such as that which occurred in 1783-4. Even though these events occur only every few hundred years, the potential for widespread loss of life means Man has to be properly prepared. As he faces continuing volcanic activity in Iceland and across the world, it is vital scientists improve eruption prediction to guard against the worst consequences.

* * * * * * *

The one certainty is that, over the course of the cycle, large parts of Earth's surface will be uninhabitable and, as we concluded in the previous chapter, experts will have to design underground towns and cities.

However, once we have constructed towns and cities underground, and linked them with Earth's core to supply heat and energy, then the interior of Earth becomes a living world. But this means we are vulnerable to changes at the core, hence someone who is bent on destroying us only has to destabilise the core.

The Devil is bent on destroying us because we are essential to the success of God's plan, and we have been virtually forced a situation where he can tempt us follow our forerunners' path to self-destruction. We can only avoid this outcome by possessing sufficient strength of character to resist his temptations. We must not allow the Devil to recreate an event that takes us back to the beginning of Time!

Chapter Six
Creating The New Jerusalem

Part 1

It is clear that we will eventually be forced into a situation where the Devil can make us face the same challenge that our forerunners failed to overcome. We can only defeat this challenge by elevating our thinking to the highest spiritual level – to reach "the third heaven" or the Hall of Judgement.

These references to the teachings of Jesus and the spiritual message that God monumentalised in the Great Pyramid show that both had foreseen this situation long ago. They also predicted victory over the Devil at the Final Conflict – the Battle of Armageddon – hence they must have equipped us with the means of achieving this victory.

The soul is the repository of our spiritual nature, and it has enormous spare capacity. The same applies to our brain. Biochemists have discovered that we are using our brains at an efficiency of only 0.41%. Since God would not have created anything surplus to our requirement, He must be intending to install various programmes that endow us with more sophisticated and powerful mental processes.

We shall require powers such as telekinesis (the power of mind over matter) and levitation (the power to free matter from the restraint of gravity) in order to recreate the object God had designed. We shall also have to be distributed throughout the universe, and therefore we require an extension to the internet facility that allows us to communicate with God so that we can speak to each other across the universe.

Our emails – thoughts – do not have mass, so their speed is not constrained by Einstein's Theory of Relativity. They can travel beyond the speed of light, to an infinitely great speed. Radiating into space at such a speed, they would reach the other side of the universe and return in an instant. Imagine being on our home planet and, at practically the same moment in time, on the other side of the universe!

However, we have shown that for each increase in our mental strength, God installed a mechanism that acts as a moral restraint, so that we raise both our mental and spiritual thinking. This means God will have to make physiological improvements to our brains that will assist higher intellectual functions and increase spiritual awareness. These require operations.

The operations amount to a recreation of Man, therefore he has effectively undergone a new birth, and this gives a new meaning to Jesus' statement, "Except [Man] be converted, and become as little children, [he] cannot enter the kingdom of Heaven" (Matthew 18.3).

A new birth is equivalent to a resurrection, and Revelation 20.4-5 duly records the "first resurrection [consisting of] them that were beheaded for the witness of Jesus, and for the word of God." This is the "resurrection of the just" mentioned in Luke 14.13-14, hence God had foreseen this development long ago.

A new version of Man that can operate on a universal scale requires a universal realm, and it is established in Revelation 21.1,5: "And I saw a new heaven and a new earth: for the first heaven and the first earth were passed away…And he that sat upon the throne said, Behold, I make all things new."

Universal Man also requires a government that can administer on a universal scale, and Revelation 20.6 sets up the government. It consists of those who have been resurrected. They will "be priests of God and Christ, and shall reign with them a thousand years."

There is a special rôle within the government for the apostles, for Jesus had promised them they will be judges over Israel: "Ye which have followed me, in the regeneration when the Son of man shall sit in the throne of his glory, shall also sit upon the twelve thrones, judging the twelve tribes of Israel" (Matthew 19.28).

A government requires an administrative centre - capital city - and, given the nature of those that have been resurrected, it has to be a holy city, hence Revelation 21.2 says, "I John saw the holy city, the new Jerusalem, coming down from heaven."

Having resurrected "the just," God's next task is to pronounce Final Judgement on the "wicked dead." This is carried out in Revelation 20.12-14: "And I saw the dead, small and great, stand before God…and the book of life was opened…and the dead were judged according to their works." After due process, "death and hell were cast into the lake of fire," which must mean Man has reached a sufficiently high level that he need be judged no more. He has also become immortal.

This exactly fits the judicial process implicit in the Great Pyramid's Hall of Judgement and the "third heaven" that was created after Jesus' ascension. It is also entirely consistent with our theory that Final Judgement entails God evaluating the lives of all who have lived before by reference to the data He had stored on CDs ("the book of life"). As this data included images of the deceased, they would appear to stand before Him.

Part 2

Once our internet facility traverses the universe, we reach the next stage – contact with intelligent life-forms in other galaxies (or they may establish contact with us). We do not doubt the existence of such life-forms because there have been too many sightings of UFOs by too many people, including highly-trained RAF personnel, for us to dismiss them as illusory. Furthermore, their existence is a logical necessity. It is essential for God to monitor our progress, especially as we possess free will, and though He has several ways of keeping track of our progress, such as the data obtained from scanning our souls when they reach Heaven, the most valuable information would be reports based on actual sightings. Therefore we believe aliens enter our world in order to monitor our progress and report back to God.[29] This means we have

29 Evidence suggests the explosion in the region of the Stony Tunguska River, Siberia, at 7am on 30th June 1908 was an exploding alien spacecraft. According to eyewitness accounts, an elongated object brighter than the Sun and trailing clouds of multi-coloured smoke sped across the sky with an ear-splitting roar. It then exploded.
The explosion was of the order of 30 million tons of TNT, equal to the largest hydrogen bombs. Scientists say the explosion was very similar to that of an atomic bomb, especially the mushrooming cloud of smoke. Much of the energy output was in the form of concussion, heat and light – again characteristic of a nuclear explosion. The temperature of the blast was deduced to be several million degrees, and only a nuclear explosion can create such temperatures. There was evidence of radiation

nothing to fear from them. Indeed, whenever we sight them, we should be on our best behaviour!

Some people claim to have been abducted by aliens. We do not doubt the validity of their claims, because monitoring our progress must include scanning the minds of people to ascertain our moral, social and political development, as well as our overall intelligence.

Alien life-forms are intelligent, but only to the extent that creatures are intelligent. Both God and Jesus have told us we are special and unique. We are meant to supervise other life-forms, which explains why our destiny is to sit at the right hand of God. In our supervisory capacity, we have to create team spirit and maintain harmony with all beings. This means we have to respect and care for them. Consequently it is no coincidence that, at the same time as we realise we have a duty of care and protection for other species on our planet, we have acquired knowledge that enables us to begin the exploration of space.

* * * * * * *

Man's supervisory rôle restores him to the position he first occupied when God placed him on Earth and drew up the Edenic Covenant that gave him dominion over other creatures, but there is now the key difference that God has granted Man dominion over every other life-form in the universe. This calls for a revision of the Edenic Covenant. It also calls for a revision of our image or likeness with God.

The likeness now resides in our spirituality, immortality and mental powers that span the universe. Our mind has always been like the

---

sickness among domestic animals in the region, and plant life also showed signs of genetic damage.

Eyewitnesses say the object did not take the simple path from south-east to north-west but instead took a course south-south-west to north-north-east, then west-south-west to east-north-east, and then finally east-south-east to west-north-west. Experts believe these course corrections indicate that the alien crew, realising their spacecraft was about to explode, manœuvred to be over the most sparsely inhabited region when it did so.

internet, because its databases are websites linked by axons (the paths along which thoughts travel), but now these websites can be likened to galaxies in the universe where there are intelligent life-forms. Since we can contact these beings through our thoughts, the universe itself is a gigantic internet.[30] But as this mirrors the internet in our mind, then our mind encompasses the universe! But this equates to God, because His wisdom also encompasses the universe, therefore this equation is the true expression of our likeness with God.

30 This echoes the point we made on p. 54 that galaxies are linked by the channels of communication between nuclei, and these channels constitute an internet broadband facility.

CHAPTER SEVEN
THE FINAL CHALLENGE

Part 1

THE FINAL CHALLENGE IS to deal with the collapse of the universe. We believe it is heralded by the death of our planet, and the irony is that its death is brought about by the Sun, which gave it life.

In 4.5 billion years time the Sun, which has been generating energy at its core by nuclear fusion (converting hydrogen into helium) will, because of the build-up of helium 'ash', have to carry out this process in less central regions. In doing so, it will have to expand into a 'red giant' and either absorb Earth or render it uninhabitable.

At the same time the Andromeda galaxy (M31) is scheduled to merge or collide with our galaxy. Andromeda is twice the size and has twice the number of stars. It is also the major member of a close triplet that includes two satellites, M32 and NGC 205, and a loose group including M33, NGC 147 and NGC 185 as more distant members. Our galaxy is also the major member of a close triplet (the other members are the Large and Small Magellanic Clouds), consequently the collision, when it occurs, will be a clash of Titans.

The collision is only occurring because Andromeda, shortly after the explosion that created the universe, was 'nudged' from its original course. Something overrode the laws of gravity. We defined gravity

In the Beginning as commands between nuclei that are based on programmes God had written, therefore the only force that can change these programmes is God Himself!

Consequently God transmitted revised instructions in the beginning to bring about the merger between our galaxy and Andromeda. Why?

The merger will create a super-galaxy. At its centre will be one of the largest black holes in the universe. It will be created by the merger of the black hole at the centre of our galaxy, which is four million times more massive than the Sun, with the far larger black hole at the centre of Andromeda (the larger a galaxy, the larger its central black hole). The black holes have to merge because gravity will force them to the centre of the newly-created super-galaxy. The enormous increase in mass at the centre will cause the super-galaxy to spin faster, in accordance with Einstein's law that mass is another form of energy ($E=mc^2$). The greater the rate of rotation, the greater the gravitational pull, and we believe the super-galaxy will have sufficient pull to draw in nearby galaxies.

Both our triplet and the Andromeda group are in a larger grouping, the Local Group of galaxies. The group contains about 54 galaxies (including dwarf galaxies), is gravitationally centred on our galaxy and Andromeda, and forms an orbiting sphere about 10 million light years across. The orbit is gradually decaying, and in 100 billion years Local Group will merge with our galaxy.

However, we believe the merger of our triplet with the Andromeda group is intended to accelerate this process, for the force of Andromeda's impact with our triplet will propel the resulting super-galaxy close to or into the Local Group, creating a colossal galaxy with unimaginable power.

This will bring within our sphere of influence a dozen or more other groups that at present are within a radius of 30 million light years from the Local Group. This is close in astronomical terms, therefore we believe that soon there will be a full-scale merger between the Local

Group (now containing our triplet and the Andromeda group) and galaxies beyond.

These include the Virgo Cluster, which contains 1,300 (and possibly 2,000) galaxies, 98% of which are concentrated in eleven regions. However, this cluster, the Local Group, our galaxy and Andromeda are only part of the Virgo Supercluster, which contains at least 100 galaxy groups within a diameter of 110 million light years. All these will merge.

Throughout the universe, mergers or collisions between galaxies will be taking place because galaxies congregate in clusters. This clustering conforms to a hierarchical order that, as we pointed out on p. 12, stems from the hierarchical order amongst nuclei. This order was created from programmes God wrote, consequently the clustering is part of God's plan.

It is only the first stage of His plan, however. His ultimate goal is to tidy up the universe by concentrating matter in one small area, and then to restore matter to the form it originally took in the world destroyed by the Big Bang.

Therefore the next stage is to merge super-galaxies. This concentrates matter in fewer areas. It also increases the size of central black holes, a factor that, as we pointed out on p. 10, fits in with God's plan because black holes hoover up vast amounts of material.

* * * * * * *

Whether galaxies merge or collide, the result is always the same: gigantic galaxies with unimaginable power and energy.

The distances between the remaining galaxies will be in the order of billions of light years, hence the conventional theory of gravity – it is the attraction between two bodies – prevents further interaction and bars further collapse. The same would also apply to Einstein's theory that gravity is spacetime warps. But our theory of gravity – it is commands between nuclei to achieve their original alignment – covers those distances and allows further collapse. Commands are dispatched through anti-gravity channels (see p. 57), therefore Einstein's Theory of Relativity operates in reverse, and commands travel at an infinitely great speed across the universe.

Consequently the remaining galaxies will merge or collide, and eventually all that is left is one galaxy containing all the material and all the power of the cosmos.

The entire process stems from programmes God wrote and installed in nuclei, hence throughout atoms have been aligning themselves according to the genome that He encrypted in their nuclei. The alignment is complete when all that is left is one galaxy containing all the material in the universe. Thereafter Man, who has been watching the process from the safety of Heaven, can begin the task of reconstructing the object God had designed but which had been destroyed by the Big Bang.

Part 2

At this stage Man has a two-fold task. He has to construct a place where he can dwell. This means recreating the Garden of Eden in which our forerunners dwelt and which God replicated on Earth for Adam and Eve. The main task, however, is broadly similar to that which our forerunners undertook – to create an object from virtually all the matter in the universe. But to our forerunners this task was merely an engineering project based on God's blueprints, whereas we have to achieve the same result from a sea of white-hot matter swirling around the largest black hole that has ever existed.

Nevertheless, one crucial factor remains unchanged. Inside each nucleus, God's programmes are fully operational, so He can commence the task of recreating the world by adjusting their programmes.

This entails, firstly, switching off communications between nuclei so as to eliminate gravity. The absence of gravity will cause the black hole to disintegrate. It will also remove friction between atoms in the swirling cloud of matter, and this will eventually reduce the temperature of the cloud to zero.

Once these results have been achieved, God will switch on the programmes but adjust the level of communication between nuclei – the force of gravity – to that which prevailed in our forerunners' day. Thereafter Man only has to make use of his supernatural powers to recreate the Garden of Eden and carry out the construction tasks originally performed by our forerunners.

Since the Garden of Eden was a living world equivalent to planet Earth, certain atoms have to coalesce to form a world. The world requires an internal source of heat, an atmosphere, light/day and darkness/night, the Sun and the Moon. These are the bases for life. They also create the seasons – another necessity of life – and set the stage for the introduction of life.

* * * * * * *

The recreation of the Garden of Eden and the object that existed before the Big Bang completes God's analysis and His schedule. It also completes His victory over the Devil who, following his defeat at the Battle of Armageddon, had been "cast into the lake of fire and brimstone." Thereafter the Devil "shall be tormented day and night for ever and ever" (Revelation 20.10) by the thought that Man has risen above temptation, achieved his destiny and sits at God's right hand.

We have aligned the main events in Revelation with the reasons why God created Man. We have also aligned them with Man's progress and the various other time-scales in God's schedule to arrive at the true meaning of a new Jerusalem and God's victory over the Devil. Thus there can be no doubt that God correctly analysed Man's future and his destiny.

Lightning Source UK Ltd.
Milton Keynes UK
UKOW040310010513

210019UK00002B/158/P

9 781477 239346